More books from Veloce...

1½-litre GP Racing 1961-1965 (Whitelock)
AC Two-litre Saloons & Buckland Sportscars (Archibald)
Alfa Romeo 155/156/147 Competition Touring Cars (Collins)
Alfa Tipo 33 (McDonough & Collins)
Alpine & Renault – The Development of the Revolutionary Turbo F1 Car 1968 to 1979 (Smith)
Autodrome (Collins & Ireland)
Bahamas Speed Weeks, The (O'Neil)
British at Indianapolis, The (Wagstaff)
British Café Racers (Cloesen)
Bugatti Type 40 (Price)
Bugatti 46/50 Updated Edition (Price & Arbey)
Bugatti T44 & T49 (Price & Arbey)
Bugatti 57 2nd Edition (Price)
Bugatti Type 57 Grand Prix – A Celebration (Tomlinson)
Cosworth – The Search for Power (6th edition) (Robson)
Daily Mirror 1970 World Cup Rally 40, The (Robson)
Datsun Fairlady Roadster to 280ZX – The Z-Car Story (Long)
Fate of the Sleeping Beauties, The (op de Weegh/Hottendorff/op de Weegh)
Ferrari 288 GTO, The Book of the (Sackey)
Ferrari 333 SP (O'Neil)
Formula One – The Real Score? (Harvey)
Formula 5000 Motor Racing, Back then ... and back now (Lawson)
Forza Minardi! (Vigar)
Grand Prix Ferrari – The Years of Enzo Ferrari's Power, 1948-1980 (Pritchard)
Grand Prix Ford – DFV-powered Formula 1 Cars (Robson)
GT – The World's Best GT Cars 1953-73 (Dawson)
Italian Cafe Racers (Cloesen)
Jaguar E-type Factory and Private Competition Cars (Griffiths)
Lamborghini Miura Bible, The (Sackey)
Lamborghini Murciélago, The book of the (Pathmanathan)
Lamborghini Urraco, The Book of the (Landsem)
Lancia 037 (Collins)
Le Mans Panoramic (Ireland)
Lexus Story, The (Long)

Lola – The Illustrated History (1957-1977) (Starkey)
Lola – All the Sports Racing & Single-seater Racing Cars 1978-1997 (Starkey)
Lola T70 – The Racing History & Individual Chassis Record – 4th Edition (Starkey)
Lotus 18 Colin Chapman's U-turn (Whitelock)
Lotus 49 (Oliver)
Making a Morgan (Hensing)
Maserati 250F In Focus (Pritchard)
Mazda MX-5/Miata 1.6 Enthusiast's Workshop Manual (Grainger & Shoemark)
Mazda MX-5/Miata 1.8 Enthusiast's Workshop Manual (Grainger & Shoemark)
Mazda MX-5 Miata, The book of the – The 'Mk1' NA-series 1988 to 1997 (Long)
Mazda MX-5 Miata, The book of the – The 'Mk2' NB-series 1997 to 2004 (Long)
Mazda MX-5 Miata Roadster (Long)
Mazda Rotary-engined Cars (Cranswick)
Mercedes-Benz SL – R230 series 2001 to 2011 (Long)
Mercedes-Benz SL – W113-series 1963-1971 (Long)
Mercedes-Benz SL & SLC – 107-series 1971-1989 (Long)
Mercedes-Benz SLK – R170 series 1996-2004 (Long)
Mercedes-Benz SLK – R171 series 2004-2011 (Long)
Mercedes-Benz W123-series – All models 1976 to 1986 (Long)
MG, Made in Abingdon (Frampton)
MGB – The Illustrated History, Updated Fourth Edition (Wood & Burrell)
Mike the Bike – Again (Macauley)
Mitsubishi Lancer Evo, The Road Car & WRC Story (Long)
Montlhéry, The Story of the Paris Autodrome (Boddy)
Morris Minor, 70 Years on the Road (Newell)
Moto Guzzi Sport & Le Mans Bible, The (Falloon)
The Moto Guzzi Story – 3rd Edition (Falloon)
Motor Racing – Reflections of a Lost Era (Carter)
Motor Racing – The Pursuit of Victory 1930-1962 (Carter)
Motor Racing – The Pursuit of Victory 1963-1972 (Wyatt/Sears)

Motor Racing Heroes – The Stories of 100 Greats (Newman)
Motorcycle GP Racing in the 1960s (Pereira)
Motorsport In colour, 1950s (Wainwright)
N.A.R.T. – A concise history of the North American Racing Team 1957 to 1983 (O'Neil)
Nissan 300ZX & 350Z – The Z-Car Story (Long)
Nissan GT-R Supercar: Born to race (Gorodji)
Northeast American Sports Car Races 1950-1959 (O'Neil)
Porsche 911R, RS & RSR, 4th Edition (Starkey)
Porsche 930 to 935: The Turbo Porsches (Starkey)
Racing Colours – Motor Racing Compositions 1908-2009 (Newman)
Racing Line – British motorcycle racing in the golden age of the big single (Guntrip)
Rallye Sport Fords: The Inside Story (Moreton)
Rootes Cars of the 50s, 60s & 70s – Hillman, Humber, Singer, Sunbeam & Talbot, A Pictorial History (Rowe)
Rover Cars 1945 to 2005, A Pictorial History
Rover P4 (Bobbitt)
Runways & Racers (O'Neil)
RX-7 – Mazda's Rotary Engine Sportscar (Updated & Revised New Edition) (Long)
Schlumpf – The intrigue behind the most beautiful car collection in the world (Op de Weegh & Op de Weegh)
Sleeping Beauties USA – abandoned classic cars & trucks (Marek)
Speedway – Auto racing's ghost tracks (Collins & Ireland)
Subaru Impreza: The Road Car And WRC Story (Long)
This Day in Automotive History (Corey)
TT Talking – The TT's most exciting era – As seen by Manx Radio TT's lead commentator 2004-2012 (Lambert)
Two Summers – The Mercedes-Benz W196R Racing Car (Ackerson)
TWR Story, The – Group A (Hughes & Scott)
Unraced (Collins)
You & Your Jaguar XK8/XKR – Buying, Enjoying, Maintaining, Modifying – New Edition (Thorley)
Wolseley Cars 1948 to 1975 (Rowe)
Works Rally Mechanic (Moylan)

Veloce's other imprints:

www.veloce.co.uk

First published in 2002 by Gryfon Press. Veloce Classic Reprint (hardback) edition published December 2018. This (paperback) edition published March 2019 by Veloce Publishing Limited, Veloce House, Parkway Farm Business Park, Middle Farm Way, Poundbury, Dorchester DT1 3AR, England. Tel +44 (0)1305 260068 / Fax 01305 250479 / e-mail info@veloce.co.uk / web www.veloce.co.uk or www.velocebooks.com.
ISBN: 978-1-787114-94-4 UPC: 6-36847-01494-0.
©2018 & 2019 John Starkey and Veloce Publishing. All rights reserved. With the exception of quoting brief passages for the purpose of review, no part of this publication may be recorded, reproduced or transmitted by any means, including photocopying, without the written permission of Veloce Publishing Ltd. Throughout this book logos, model names and designations, etc, have been used for the purposes of identification, illustration and decoration. Such names are the property of the trademark holder as this is not an official publication. Readers with ideas for automotive books, or books on other transport or related hobby subjects, are invited to write to the editorial director of Veloce Publishing at the above address. British Library Cataloguing in Publication Data – A catalogue record for this book is available from the British Library. Typesetting, design and page make-up all by Veloce Publishing Ltd on Apple Mac. Printed and bound by CPI Group (UK) Ltd, Croydon, CR0 4YY.

Veloce *Classic Reprint* Series

NISSAN

The GTP & Group C Racecars 1984-1993

Lightning Speed

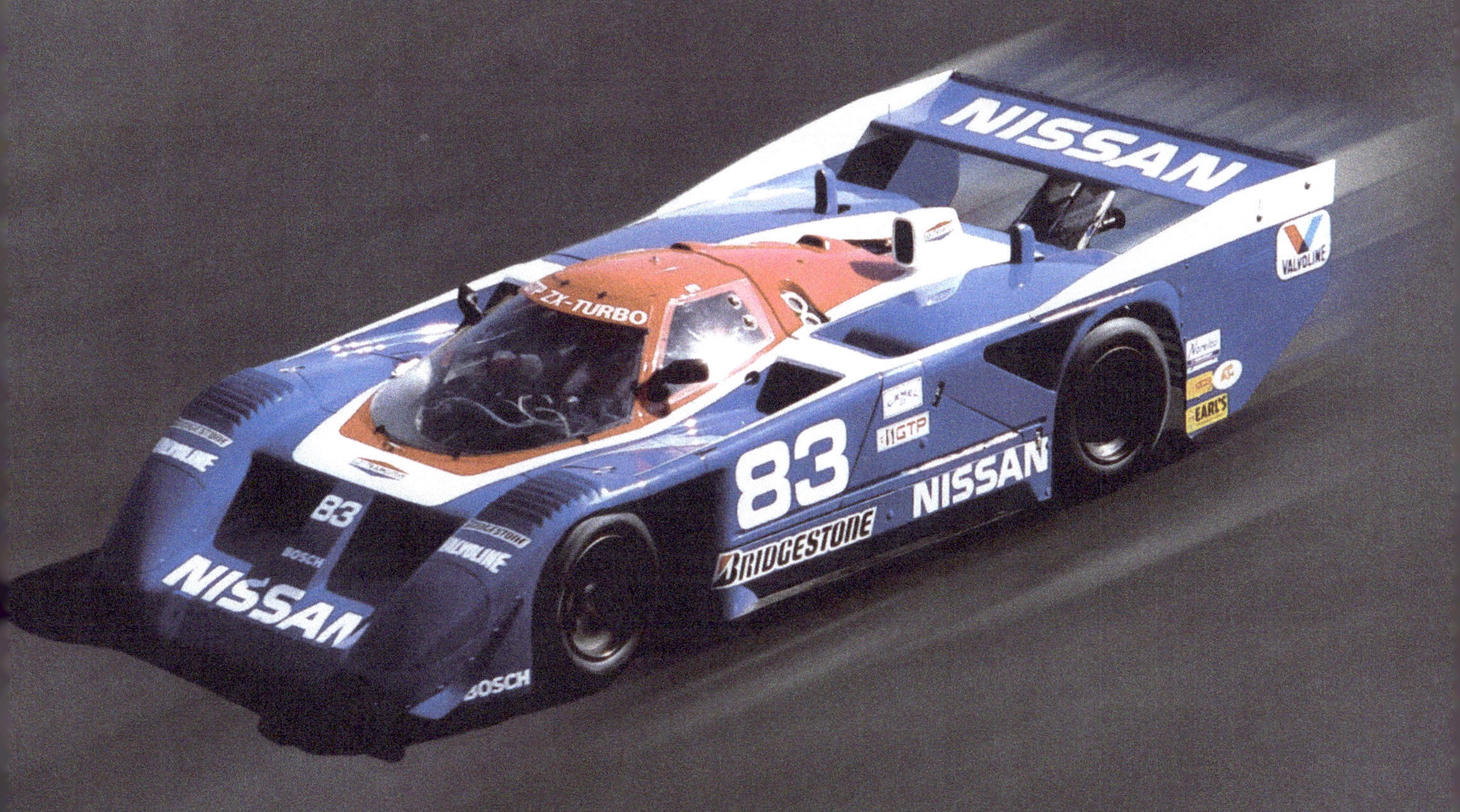

John Starkey

ACKNOWLEDGEMENTS

This was a book where, having now written some ten books on the subject of motor racing, I thought I'd let the people who participated in the events tell the story.

One thing became immediately apparent: For most of the people concerned, racing Nissans from 1985 to 1993 was one of the most exciting times of their working lives. The enthusiasm poured out. And why not? These cars were at the very forefront of the racing technology of their day. They were unbelievably fast. Consider that, as of 2002, a Nissan still holds the Le Mans lap record – Mark Blundell doing the honors in 1990. It has not yet (2002) been beaten. And this was with the chicanes on the Mulsanne straight. Thanks for your reminiscences, Mark. Thanks also to Julian Bailey, Mark's co-driver. And to Kenny Acheson who, coming from the all-conquering Sauber-Mercedes team, called the Nissans: "The best of the rest." Thanks to Dave Price, that doyen of team managers, plus his assistant, Bob Bell. Dave Scotney, Lola's Chief Engineer, and Laurie Bray, Lola's Archivist, thank you all for your memories of the European Group C Nissans.

Electramotive. Who can forget that name, which is indelibly linked to Nissan's racing success in the States? Don Devendorf, John Knepp, Geoff Brabham, John Morton, Elliott Forbes-Robinson, Hurley Haywood, Yoshi Suzuki, Ashley Page, Curt Geatches, Wes Moss, Trevor Harris, Kas Kastner, Don Reynolds, Frank Honsowitz. All gave freely of their time to talk about what were, indubitably, great days for Sportscar and GT racing.

Today, the Nissan GTP and Group C cars are being raced avidly by a bunch of hard-charging and skilled drivers in HSR events. People like Toby Bean, Charlie Agg, Michael Lauer, Jim Oppenheimer, Benton Bryan, Mike Lattos, Paul Reisman, Brian deVries and Peter Racely. They are looked after and maintained enthusiastically by such skilled people as Steve Kibble, Richard Brown, Jerry Archer, Chuck White and the Bennetts – Bud, Kurt and Craig. I thank you one and all.

DEDICATION

To Don Devendorf,

A Truly Enlightened Engineer

TABLE OF CONTENTS

ACKNOWLEDGEMENTS	....	iv
FOREWORD	....	vi
INTRODUCTION	....	vii
CHAPTER ONE	ELECTRAMOTIVE THE AMERICAN NISSANS	1
CHAPTER TWO	1990 – NPTI	48
CHAPTER THREE	THE EUROPEAN GROUP C NISSANS	64
CHAPTER FOUR	1990 WORLD CHAMPIONSHIP	90
CHAPTER FIVE	NISSAN RACING IN JAPAN	120
APPENDIX	....	143

FOREWORD

I've raced many cars during my career. One of the first things that any racing driver learns is the importance of both the equipment and the team of people who look after the car. I doubt there's ever been a racecar with a continuous run of success, such as the Nissan GTP that I drove in the late eighties and early nineties, that's not had both of these attributes.

Certainly, the Nissan GTP cars, with the Trevor Harris designed chassis were very fast; they were easy to set up and always had great traction; and John Caldwell's engines were not only powerful but also very reliable. However, none of these attributes would have made the Nissan the winner it became, without the superb engineering backup plus the dedication and expertise of the Electramotive/NPTI crew who gave me a racecar that rarely ever failed. Throw in great pit stops and what more could a driver possibly want.

When I was first asked to drive for Electramotive (which became NPTI in 1990) in 1985, I declined. I'd seen the car have a bad crash when something broke and didn't want to drive it. Fortunately, Trevor Harris (with whom I went back to the time of the VDS Lola T530 in 1980) persuaded me to test the car and the potential was very obvious as soon as I drove it. But it was the "we will win" attitude of the Kas Kastner led team that impressed me the most, and I really felt that these guys could and would do the job of winning the IMSA Camel GT Championship.

That we did win is a tribute to the team's ingenuity and hard work. It is also a tribute to Nissan's faith in the team. I like to think that we repaid that faith by winning the Championship for four straight years, 1988-91.

GEOFF BRABHAM

INTRODUCTION

A great era of racing took place in the eighties and early nineties. Blindingly fast GTP and Group C cars were created to run on either side of the Atlantic and the Pacific. They battled it out across America, Europe and Japan.

In Europe, these latter day Sports-prototypes, with their genesis being the Porsche 917's, Ferrari 512's and Lola T70's of the late 1960's, gained ground effects, turbocharging and, later on, electronically controlled engine management systems to make the most of every last drop of fuel allocated.

This latter innovation was important for cars needing to make pitstops and take on fuel. It was especially important for the Group C prototypes of Europe and Japan, where a fuel allocation formula was in force, making a necessity of frugality, combined with speed.

In America, John Bishop's IMSA sanctioning body would have nothing to do with the European idea of fuel allocation, but that didn't stop a brilliant electronics engineer, Don Devendorf, from developing his own, highly superior electronic engine management system, arguably the finest of its day.

And to which car did Don Devendorf's company, Electramotive, fit this electronic marvel? Why, a Nissan. It was Devendorf who brought Nissan to the fore in International racing, winning them three straight IMSA Championships. Of course, under the skin, the car was a much-developed Lola with a Hewland gearbox and an engine built by Electramotive but with Nissan footing the bill.

In Europe and at home, Nissan commissioned March Engineering of Bicester, England to build Group C Sports-prototypes from 1983 onwards and then switched to Lola chassis in 1989 and 1990 in their quest to win Le Mans. They may have failed in that particular endeavor, but they left their mark: The fastest qualifying lap ever at Le Mans, in 1990.

These were, and are, great cars. Very powerful, with over 1000 horsepower on occasions, very fast, endowed with the greatest downforce of any of these cars and with an aura about them that reeked of serious intent.

JOHN STARKEY

ELECTRAMOTIVE
The American Nissans

Victory once again for the Nissan GTP ZX-Turbo in their incredible run of success in 1988.
[Photo: Courtesy of Ashley Page.]

NISSAN: THE GTP & GROUP C RACECARS 1984-1993

Nissans have been raced for far longer than most people think, and those who raced them have stayed remarkably true to the marque. In 1971 the BRE Datsun team comprised: John Morton and Pete Brock as drivers (John also worked as a fabricator with BRE); John Caldwell, who built the engines, and John Knepp, who looked after the gearboxes. The engineer in charge of the suspension was Trevor Harris. Yoshi Suzuka also worked for BRE. All of these people would stay with Nissans and later take part in their triumph in GTP racing, employed by Electramotive.

Hand-in-hand with the commercial success of Datsun's 240Z in the States came success on the racetracks. Various 240Zs were modified to take part in the GTU (Grand Touring Under 2.5-liters) class of IMSA, starting in 1973. The most notable of these were driven by Bob Sharp, Paul Newman, Sam Posey, and a young electronics engineer, then employed by the Hughes aircraft company of California, named Don Devendorf.

Don Devendorf and his friend, fellow racer and partner in the venture, John Knepp, started Electramotive Engineering of California in 1974. Knepp had his shop situated very closely to Don Devendorf's place, and the pair had long known each other.

John Knepp, in an interview with the author, recalled: "I actually started with Pete Brock's team in 1969. We developed the two-liter roadster, the 510 and the Z car. We also built a pick-up and went drag racing!

Pete Brock lost interest in racing and went hang-gliding, and so I started Electramotive Engineering. Dick Roberts of Nissan had had his eye on Don Devendorf, as he was a rising star on the racetrack. We worked out a deal, built a B210, and Don won the SCCA Championship with it."

Trevor Harris, later to be so instrumental as Electramotive's 'in house' designer, remembered: "In 1972, Nissan developed their little sedan, the 1200. They asked me to design a rear suspension package for a private driver. That driver turned out to be Don Devendorf. He won pole position and every race that year in his SCCA division."

Don Devendorf mortgaged his house to provide funds to start Electramotive. There were two companies housed under one roof: Electramotive Engineering being the race team (75% owned by Don Devendorf), whilst Electramotive Inc. was the engineering side (75% owned by John Knepp).

Electramotive became America's leading specialist in the sale and preparation of road and racing Nissans, and when the Japanese company decided to enter the GTP category, they naturally approached

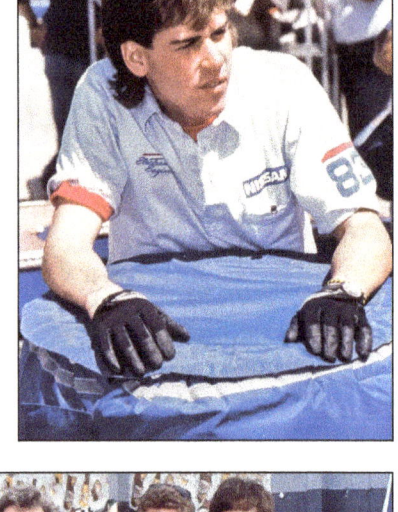

Clockwise (from above):
Don Devendorf with his wife, Alice, and their children.
Trevor Harris, the gifted designer, and his wife, Freddie. Note the T-shirts.
Mike Ferrari, Electramotive's tire engineer. On the back of this photo, Ashley Page wrote: "The Best!"
Road America, 1988. Four of the Nissan's Electramotive crew take time out for a photo. From left, they are: Hersey Mallory, Joe Tobin, Kevin Scham and Ray Guna. Wes Moss and John Christie.
[Photos: Courtesy of Ashley Page.]

Devendorf to run the project. First of all, Devendorf approached March Engineering of Bicester, England, but they had too many commitments to be able to supply what Electramotive needed.

Don Devendorf: "We were doubtful about March's capacity to design in enough cooling for a turbo car. Having run the Nissan straight-six engine up to 8500 rpm for 24 hours, we knew how much cooling the new V6 engine would need in turbocharged form. March had never really succeeded in making their turbocharged engines in their Group C and GTP cars last, but Eric Broadley of Lola was fully cognizant of this requirement and willing to design a chassis around the engine."

So Electramotive then contacted March's rival, Lola, and commissioned Eric Broadley, the owner and chief designer, to design and build the T810 rolling chassis, which was based on a T710 monocoque, the tubs built for GM for their 'Corvette GTP' project. The T810 had slightly different detail modifications (to the T710) to allow for the Nissan engine, cooling and bodywork installations. The two chassis shared similar suspension installations and physical dimensions.

Trevor Harris, later to figure most prominently in the Nissan/Electramotive story commented: "When Lola did the T810, Nissan was led to believe that the car was unique, however, a lot of that car was interchangeable with the T710 Corvette GTP car. Our project must have been a real profit center for Lola."

The Lola T810 was designed by Eric Broadley and Clive Lark. In Electramotive Nissan form, the car ran under the name Nissan GTP ZX Turbo. There were four chassis originally built by Lola.

A front view of the first Electramotive Nissan GTP ZX Turbo (Lola T810) in the Lola factory awaiting paint. [Photo: Courtesy of Ashley Page.]

Two of the T810s were delivered to the Le Mans Company in Japan for use in the Japanese Sportscar Championship. The other two, sent from Lola on April 11th and May 15th 1985 to Electramotive, had been assembled by, amongst others, Laurie Bray.

Laurie, who has been with Lola since the its inception, (he is today the company's historian and archivist) remembered: "That was a very difficult car to build. We were given dummy Nissan engines and worked around them in the chassis. I remember the water-cooling pipes having to be armored as the water pressure system used the then unheard of pressure of 60 psi. And the fuel pumps! There seemed to be batteries of them."

"Another problem that we had was with the bodywork. Because carbon fiber was so new, we used the same sort of moulds that we had used previously for fiberglass bodywork. After the first body had been built, the moulds shifted. I had the devil of a job to make the bodywork fit the second, third and fourth cars made!"

Ashley Page of North Carolina became Electramotive's first Crew Chief in 1984. "When I started with Electramotive, the Lola was not even started on. John Bright, when he had worked at Lola, did a great deal of work on the T600 and I flew to England with him and we had to finish the car up in the factory."

John Knepp: "We (Electramotive) had contracted with Nissan, Japan, to supply their Marches and the Le Mans Company's T810s, with V6 race engines. The engine used a single Garrett TO3 turbocharger and our own fuel-injection system. By 1985, we were already getting close to a thousand horsepower from the V6."

Don Devendorf (left) with Ashley Page. [Photo: Courtesy of Ashley Page.]

"I remember that when the team went to the first race, Ashley Page watched them as they left and said: 'Look at 'em all gung-ho. They think they're going to win

The first Lola T810 arrives at Electramotive's shop in April 1985. [Photo: Courtesy of Ashley Page.]

straight away. They don't realize what you have to go through to make a project like this work'."

The monocoque tub of the Lola T810 was fabricated from flat aluminum honeycomb panels, but the floor had carbon fiber skins for increased rigidity. The honeycomb pontoons flanking the cockpit added extra strength. The bodywork was glass pre-preg on aluminum and non-metallic Nomex honeycomb, depending on the complexity of shape in the area used. The venturi-shaped underbody was of a sandwich structure, using glass pre-preg and carbon fiber strategically.

The engine was supported by a tubular steel frame, and this was bolted to the bulkhead. The front suspension was of the twin A-arm variety, with pushrods operating the front suspension from the coil spring/damper units, which were crossed over in the scuttle area to make room for the cooling air channels. The conventional rear suspension was by wishbones and outboard coil spring/damper units. Brakes were 13

The Weismann transverse gearbox. [Photo: Courtesy of Ashley Page.]

inch ventilated discs and AP four-pot calipers were fitted. A Weismann 5-speed transverse gearbox was used initially.

Don Devendorf: "When we started on the GTP project, there was really only the old Hewland LG600 gearbox that we could buy from them. The LG600 was a strong gearbox, but the gear change was too slow. That's why we went with the Weismann. The Weismann was a transverse gearbox with a very short input shaft. Later, Hewland brought out the VGC gearbox, and that was the gearbox we wound up using. Unlike the Weismann, the Hewland was a longitudinal design and had a long input shaft that smoothed out the power pulses from the engine on their way to the rear end."

Don Devendorf: "The T810 had been designed using a static wind tunnel. Lola's bodywork created extreme sensitivity to ride height, making the car unstable under braking. The only cure was to spring it very stiffly."

The Lola T810 awaiting finishing and despatch to Electramotive, whilst at the Lola factory. Laurie Bray recounted that, at the last moment, they realized that no wiper arm had been designed for the car and so the wiper from the Ford Transit van in the background was taken off and fitted to the Lola for shipment to the U.S.A! [Photo: Courtesy of Ashley Page.]

The GTP ZXT's potential was not realized in the first season, as Devendorf's car was twice written off, once when its suspension broke on a super-speedway banking, and it was also crashed badly in an incident at Elkhart Lake.

Don Devendorf: "Well, one crash, the whole side of the bell-housing pulled

The Lola T810's monocoque chassis. Of honeycomb aluminum, reinforced with carbon fiber floors, it was strong for its day but difficult to work on. [Photo: Courtesy of Ashley Page.]

The fastest of all the GTP drivers, Geoff Brabham, pictured with his wife, Rosina. [Photo: Courtesy of Ashley Page.]

out. I remember that, at Laguna Seca, I was going around and felt something shaking. I pulled into the pits and we found the front axle had broken. Another time, the front bulkhead split."

Trevor Harris, later to design the chassis of the successful 1988 car remembered Don testing the GTP car: "Don had a black box that ran the injection. It was the only one, hand built by Don. It had survived several crashes. Don was a real hands-on guy and built this box at home."

"I can remember running tests with Don as driver in '86. I'll never, never forget wondering what in the world I was doing, as Don pulls into the pits, jumps out and pulls the box out. Then he would run into the trailer and change resistors and capacitors. He knew what was happening inside it, besides driving the car. Very few drivers can do that, but he knew what to do."

The electronic engine control processor (or EECP as it was known) was Don Devendorf's own particular contribution to the engine balance of horsepower and torque plus fuel

Above: The Nissan V6 engine as used in the 1985-89 GTP cars. Of V6 configuration, it proved incredibly powerful, developing upwards of 1000 horsepower in qualifying trim and 800 horsepower in the races themselves. All this with complete reliability, once Electramotive had switched to an aluminum block in place of the original steel one. Up to the end of 1989, the original heads were used. [Photo: Courtesy of Ashley Page.]

Above – The front view of the Electramotive-tuned Nissan V6 engine. [Photo: Courtesy of Ashley Page.]

Below – Power generates heat. The Nissan V6 engine, in turbocharged form, required enormous coolers to keep it alive. Pictured here, their size can be appreciated. [Photo: Courtesy of Ashley Page.]

consumption. Don, Brent Dussia, Eugene Franciscus and the rest of the Electramotive electronics laboratory were responsible for the creation of this engine management system that contributed so much to Nissan's success. The EECP had actually started life on Don's GTU car and was refined and developed from there.

In the spring of 1986, the newly signed driver-pairing of Elliott Forbes-Robinson and Geoff Brabham suddenly appeared on the front row of the grid for

The Electramotive "Nissan GTP ZX Turbo" made its debut at Riverside in 1985. It practiced, but did not start due to gearbox failure. [Photo: Courtesy of Ashley Page.]

the Riverside 6 hours race alongside the pole-sitting Buick Hawk (nee March) of John Paul, Jr. Both were superb road racers and their arrival enabled Don Devendorf to concentrate completely upon developing the car still further.

Trevor Harris: "I worked with Geoff from 1980 on and thought that he was just terrific. So when Wes (Moss) called me for drivers' suggestions in early 1986, I called Geoff Brabham. He was worried about the history of unreliability of the Electramotive Nissan GTP effort. But he did a test, liked it and did the last two races of the season."

Geoff Brabham: "When I was first asked to drive the Nissan GTP car, I said no. I had seen the car hit the wall at Pocono with Don Devendorf driving. The seatbelt anchorages had torn out, and there was Don, totally winded, lying on the grass beside the car. It really put me off."

"Anyway, Trevor persevered with asking Kas Kastner to pursue me to drive for Electramotive and I went to have a look at their operation. It was then that I realized that they did have a handle on the problems, so I signed with them."

Brabham and Forbes-Robinson had undertaken an extensive testing and development program for Electramotive in the preceding month and this was now paying dividends. Their race at Riverside, however, was soon over, when Brabham crashed in the first hour.

Geoff Brabham: "The first time I raced the car was at Riverside and I can remember pulling into pitlane with all the crew clapping their hands. 'Great.' I thought. 'We're on pole.' When they opened the door, it was to tell me we were second!"

"In the race itself, the steering broke going into turn one and I hit the wall in turn two. The steering broke on the left hand side, so I got through turn one, but then there was no steering for the next turn and I just brushed the wall. I wasn't very impressed."

At Laguna Seca, Elliott Forbes-Robinson took provisional pole position on the Saturday in the re-energized team's lead car, carrying race #83. In the last qualifying session, EFR was "bumped" down to third place on the grid, but still wound up tenth overall, after the differential broke.

Electramotive again resorted to testing in the middle of the summer, developing new bodywork for the nose, in the rear and a new underwing, too. The team's aerodynamic thinking was drifting away from the full-length venturi tunnel approach of the Group C type outlook.

Yoshi Suzuka, the team's aerodynamicist: "My favorite design was what we called the '86 and a 1/2' bodywork. This gave us more downforce than we had ever had previously. I redesigned the front diffuser and even though the front looked the same as the Lola, it wasn't really. The cockpit also looked the same, but all the rear bodywork and the venturis were new." By mid-86, two cars were being used and the

12

At Electramotive, the crew, with Ashley Page, Wes Moss and Yoshi Suzuka amongst them, inspects the newly painted Nissan GTP ZX Turbo, nee Lola T810. [Photo: Courtesy of Ashley Page.]

Left:
Tony Adamowicz (nearest camera) and Don Devendorf standing by the original Nissan GTP ZX Turbo whilst testing in 1985.

Below:
The Nissan GTP ZX Turbo on the track in 1985, early on in the car's life.

[Photos: Courtesy of Ashley Page.]

new, revised bodywork was evident to the perceptive eye.

The Nissan GTP ZX Turbo came back to racing with a bang. Geoff Brabham put the car on pole for the Portland sprint race, pipping the T710 Corvette, and would have won but for a last minute splash-and-dash pitstop for fuel when seven seconds

Above – The "California Coolers"-sponsored car being tested at Riverside in 1985.

Below – The car on test at Riverside. Another view of it being worked on with Ashley Page heading operations in this photograph.

The water-cooled, electronically controlled, twin wastegate with twin pop-off valves atop the turbocharger. The oil sump is visible at the bottom of this photograph. This also served as the mounting on the bellhousing. The tailpipe exhausted into the underbody tunnels that were used in the Nissan GTP ZX Turbo.
[Photo: Courtesy of Ashley Page.]

in the lead. He dropped to third, Holbert's Porsche taking the win but even that was by far the car's best result to date. It turned out that the fuel capacity of the Nissan had not been enough to finish the race. A quick change to larger fuel cells occurred the very next week.

This performance was no flash in the pan. The car again shared the front row with the Corvette at Road Atlanta, was in the third slot in Watkins Glen, and was back to pole position in Columbus with the 'Vette beside it. In the races, however, they were not in luck, and further podiums eluded them for the rest of the season.

Don Devendorf: "I worked for Hughes, who were bought by Raytheon who, in turn, were bought by GM. I used to think it amusing that the new managers never asked me to help on the Corvette project. I guess they thought there may have been a conflict of interest. At the racetracks, I would see the GM engineers trying to solve problems on the Corvette that we'd already worked through. In particular, they had a problem with ignition shielding that we'd solved already."

"Electramotive was a very good team of people. Engineers are there to solve problems, and that's why we built our own solutions. I guess that you could say that the Nissan GTP car was a triumph of development over design, although Lola were very co-operative."

John Knepp's company, as we have seen, developed the turbo V6 engines, based upon the production 'Z' car engine. These were now built in-house by Don Reynolds, and featured a new aluminum block and aluminum heads. John Knepp's team, under

Don Reynolds, designed, developed and reprogrammed the engine's sophisticated electronic management unit. It was during 1987 that John Knepp took the first step towards developing what became one of Electramotive's strongest assets in winning the IMSA Camel GT Championship, the electronically controlled turbocharger wastegate.

John Knepp: "Well, the trouble with the spring-loaded wastegate was that as soon as the boost started rising (in the turbocharger circuit), the wastegate would start to open, and you'd lose all the boost. I worked out a pneumatically-controlled wastegate that held the 'gate shut until it really needed to open, and called in Don to watch the engine perform on our dyno."

"We had a test rig that simulated full throttle shifts with the engine running and Don was impressed. We estimated that this alone knocked a tenth of a

The Lola-Nissan, now in red, white and blue livery, instead of the previous black. The new, Yoshi Suzuka-designed bodywork is fitted, superseding the original Lola T810 shape. [Photo: Courtesy of Ashley Page.]

NISSAN: THE GTP & GROUP C RACECARS 1984-1993

Pitstop time. Kas Kastner is nearest the camera on the right. [Photo: Courtesy of Ashley Page.]

second off each corner. Don said 'Let's do this electronically' and set to work. He's a World-class guy when it comes to electronics."

"As soon as we had to use restrictors, we started downsizing the turbocharger, to improve reaction time. We had started the engine development with a big single-turbocharger. As we developed and tested the car, we went to a medium, and then an even smaller turbo. At each change, the car lapped faster. Top speed fell from 220 to 170 plus mph but the cornering speed went up and up as the downforce grew greater. Our engines put out some 750 foot pounds of torque. The car grew quite draggy with all

Right – Wes Moss tends to the rear suspension of the Lola T810. The Weismann gearbox's transverse gears can be seen besides the CV shaft. [Photo: Courtesy of Ashley Page.]

Yoshi Suzuka watching the Nissan being tested at Riverside. [Photo: Courtesy of Ashley Page.]

that downforce, but it had the power to pull it out of corners. We went 2-3 seconds a lap faster with the restrictors, but using the electronic wastegate."

John Borgan was the head of Nissan's operation in America and, in early 1986, he had asked Kas Kastner to help with Electramotive's dealings with Nissan in Japan. Kastner started work in February 1986 and immediately told the Corporation that Electramotive would bring them the IMSA Camel GTP Championship if they were left to get on with the engineering side. Nissan agreed and sent Electramotive the funds needed in order to develop the Lola-Nissan into an effective winner on the tracks.

It was at this time, due to Kastner's insistence, that the cars, which had previously appeared painted black with "California Cooler" sponsorship, became red, white and blue, with "Nissan" shown prominent on the flanks.

"When I started in February 1986," recalled Kastner, "the people put in charge of the racing management at Nissan were not up to the demands that Electramotive placed on them."

"I knew Don Devendorf from way

Chassis Number 8701 (Elvis) being serviced in preparation for the IMSA Camel GT race at Laguna Seca in 1987. [Photo: Courtesy of Ashley Page.]

Nissan: The GTP & Group C Racecars 1984-1993

The Nissan ZX GTP in 1987. [Photo: Courtesy of Ashley Page.]

Top & Center – The Trevor Harris-designed chassis of 1988. [Photo: Courtesy of Ashley Page.]

Bottom – The new, conventional and simpler front suspension of the 1988 Trevor Harris chassis. [Photo: Courtesy of Ashley Page.]

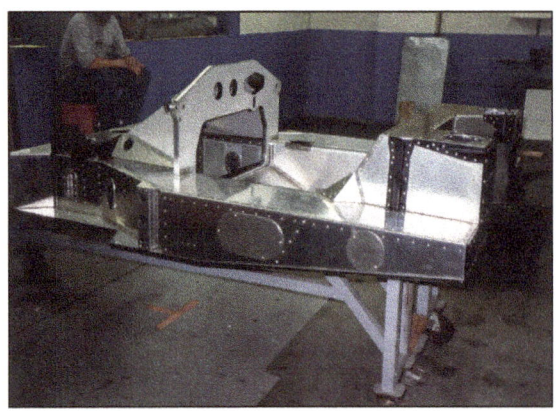

back, so he and I were friends. He had won a Championship in a Triumph *(cont. pg 30)* Spitfire when I was running Triumph racing in the States. After Triumph, I went on with my own company to race in Can Am, Formula 5000 and Indy. When it's your own dollars, you don't suffer fools gladly!"

"So, Nissan were upside down with this program and nothing could get done. Don and Wes Moss were great engineers but they were not managers. It was actually an old friend from Triumph days who called me. 'Do you know anyone who could be our Motor Sports Manager?' he asked. I had just sold my company and wasn't doing anything. I asked them to consider me and was promptly given the job. When I went to meet Nissan USA's then CEO, Tom Mignanelli, we reached an understanding within twenty minutes. Basically, I told him: 'Give me the dough and I'll get the job done'."

The effort was in full swing by

Finally! 1987 and the Nissan receives the Hewland VGZ longitudinal gearbox to replace the unreliable Weismann transmission. [Photo: Courtesy of Ashley Page.]

1987, development being frantic and ongoing. At Miami in early 1987, the car won at last. Brabham and Forbes-Robinson took the pole and beat Rahal and Mass' Porsche 962 in chassis number 8701 ("Elvis").

Don Reynolds: "That car got fitted with the wrong engine. Wes Moss, the team manager, called and asked me which engine to fit and I gave him the engine number to use over the 'phone. When I got to the circuit, I took a look and said: 'Holy Christ, this is the oldest engine we've got!' That engine must have done over fifty hours of running. Well in the race, everything was going fine until fifteen minutes before the end, when Geoff (Brabham) came on the radio to tell us that the oil pressure at high revs was fading. I told Wes to tell him to turn the boost all the way down. When we looked at the engine afterwards, the block was cracked. Another lap, and the crankshaft woulda fallen out!"

Electramotive Nissans took four more pole positions but no more victories that season. The Nissans were fast but unreliable.

Kas Kastner again: "The first thing we did was to change the color from black to red, white and blue. Black is for when you've already kicked ass."

"To my mind, there were two major things in turning the effort around. One was getting the new gearbox, and the other was getting Geoff Brabham. I have a lot of respect for Geoff. He's always spot on with everything he does and his driving is dead smooth. He's always race fit, too. When he goes out for a quick lap, you don't have to wait till lap three or four, he's already done it on lap one."

By 1987 the revisions to the bodywork had doubled the original car's downforce at 200 mph. The car's competitiveness was also helped by new rules restricting its turbocharged opposition to the same 3-liter capacity.

Don Devendorf: "Yoshi *(Suzuka – Author)*, designed new bodywork in our wind tunnel, which gave the car a wide

Electramotive produced all its own special bodywork for their car in a dedicated bodyshop attached to their plant in El Segundo. Here is that shop in 1988 with body panels stacked against the wall. [Photo: Courtesy of Ashley Page.]

range of compliance. As well, we had gone from twin to a single turbocharger and changed over to Goodyear tires. The Bridgestones were so much slower. Of course, the Goodyear engineers had been at the races too, looking after their other customers. They had long ago worked out that we would be faster with their tires."

"I remember testing at Riverside with the 'new' 1988 set-up that the IMSA rules forced upon us with inlet restrictors. Now we had less top-end horsepower and there were two fast sections at Riverside where we were two seconds slower than in the previous year. But, with the bodywork changes and the turbo's electronic wastegate, and the new Goodyears, we were two seconds faster per lap overall than the previous year."

Elliott Forbes-Robinson: "Well, Don (Devendorf) and I went way back in SCCA racing. I was really fortunate to get the chance to get together with him again as a driver with the Electramotive Nissans. I was also unlucky enough to start with the Lola-Nissan. Then Electramotive came out with their own version of that and it was so great to drive. Don had done a great job with it. He really was so far ahead of the other teams, especially where technical matters were concerned. John Knepp had got the engine to where there was no turbo lag at all."

"Electramotive were such a great

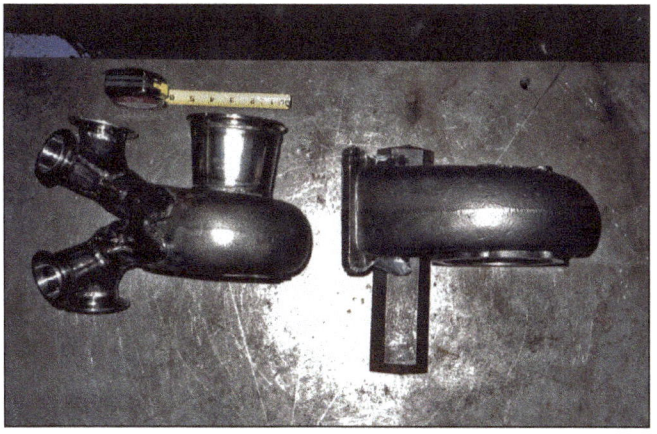

These photos illustrate the meticulous work carried out by AIR on the Nissan's turbochargers. Side-by-side can be seen the original turbocharger and, following AIR's work, a polished, lightened turbocharger with mountings for the electronic wastegate. [Photo: Courtesy of Ashley Page.]

team. For example, they would come out with a new rear wing and the engineer would say: 'I think you should mount it at, say, five degrees rake.' We'd go out and test and, you know what? After trying all sorts of angles, we'd finish up with the wing at exactly five degrees after testing it, the same as the engineer had figured out in the wind tunnel!"

"Anyway, the problem while I was there was Bridgestone tires, which kept on

Above: Even in the pouring rain, testing went on. [Photos: Courtesy of Ashley Page.]

Opposite page: Top – One of the Nissans with the Trevor Harris-designed chassis in 1988. Compare to the photograph of "Elvis": The chassis attitude in the corner is exactly the same.
Bottom – One of the Lola-chassis'd cars, probably "Elvis", chassis number 8701, seen cornering hard in 1988.

blowing out. I had at least three let go on me, one of them really serious, at Riverside in testing. I was scared. Bridgestone just didn't have a handle on why it happened then, even though they've come on a lot since."

"I went over and talked to the Hendrick team about driving their Corvettes for them at the end of 1987 and came back to tell Kas Kastner that I had to leave unless they could do something about the tires. Kas said: 'No, sorry, we're staying with Bridgestones'. One month later, Don called to say that Electramotive had signed a new contract with Goodyears and would I come back please? I had just signed with Chevrolet for the Corvette and had to refuse. So I went to the Corvette team and discovered that Don and the Electramotive team were light years ahead of Chevrolet, especially when it came to the fuel injection."

"I really would have loved to stay with Don, Geoff and Kas at Electramotive. They were such a great team. I drove a Nissan ZX-GTP recently at Elkhart Lake and found once again what a super car it was. No turbo lag. What a great car."

Kas Kastner remembered about the tire situation: "Well, Bridgestone treated us as second cousins really. They liked Porsches and, at Riverside, I remember they only brought two spare tires. Don would complain but he wasn't getting anywhere and in 1986 we had to use Bridgestone's bias ply tires but for 1987 we had to reconfigure all our suspension to take their radial tires. I remember that, at Riverside, Elliott had a big accident but it turned out later that he had run over a broken turbine wheel that had been deposited there by a Porsche blow-up. The car was junk and that cost us $100,000. Finally, Bridgestone said that they would take back the radials and we would have to use their bias ply tires. 'We're going to Formula One next year,' was what we were told and that's when we changed to Goodyears. We also knew that the Jaguars were coming in 1988 and they were on Dunlop tires, so Goodyear were very keen to help us."

"The Weismann gearbox was an engineering marvel and Joe Tobin and Wes Moss did all they could to solve the problems that it kept on throwing up. Gear sets kept failing and the reason turned out to be that every gear ratio had to have its own special shim set. Running the Weismann transmission was very expensive! At this time, Hewland came out with their new VG gearbox and that solved our transmission problems."

In late 1987, Jim Chapman's JC Prototypes company built a new chassis, designed by Trevor Harris, to take the older car's running gear and bodywork. Principally, this new chassis featured a stronger floor plus a completely new, simpler front suspension layout that left the coil spring/damper units outboard of the chassis for easier servicing.

Trevor Harris: "Kas Kastner came to visit me in 1987. A complex situation

Geoff Brabham steers the Nissan to victory at Miami.

had arisen at Electramotive. The cars were fast but unreliable. They were thinking of designing a whole new car, and Kas asked me what direction I thought Nissan should go in."

"I said, 'No, you don't need a new car. The engine is good, the bodywork is good. What you need is a new, updated chassis, one with a simpler front end.' The original T810 front suspension was extremely hard to work on, miserable. 'I can design a new chassis to fit under the bodywork. I can probably make a stiffer chassis, too.' The original Lola chassis wasn't very stiff. The rear suspension was reasonably acceptable. That saved a lot of money, and we also saved the front uprights, but I designed different pick up points for them. That changed the front suspension to a simple thing. My geometry was quite different, too, just a designer preference. The new suspension had much better geometry. If you look at the original 1985 Lola and 1988 Nissan GTP car, there is no connection."

"That's what happened. Kas hired me separately from Electramotive to design a new chassis. As I said, that project came up in 1987. There was a real time crunch. It was a big rush to get all the parts made but, for 1988, we had a car that looked similar to the year before, but was very different under the skin."

Below:
John Morton with Sylvia Wilkerson, Electramotive timekeeper and John's long time companion.
[Photo: Courtesy of Ashley Page.]

Left:
Not all was work, work, work. This is Penthouse "Pet of the Year" on the grid at Watkins Glen in 1987.
[Photo: Courtesy of Ashley Page.]

"The 1988 car was a very reliable tank. The chassis was easy to work on, spring changes could be done in three minutes. Before, they had taken an hour. I engineered the lead car for Geoff Brabham. We'd do a lot of spring changes over a weekend. The other teams couldn't match us."

Kas Kastner: "I talked to Trevor Harris, Lola and our other engineers about the new chassis idea and then commissioned Trevor to do it. Trevor wouldn't take help but I had to find out how much tooling we needed and, in a meeting with Trevor and John Chapman, they gave me May 15th as their deadline, so I had to find the money for that. I did it by making a presentation to Nissan USA's Vice-Presidents to get part of next year's budget to finance that. It was only recently that one of their senior Vice-Presidents told me that he had received instructions to kill the whole project. Luckily, I managed to talk them round it."

Geoff Brabham: "When Yoshi Suzuka totally re-did the bodywork, I can remember feeling the difference as I drove out of pitlane, it was that much better. When the Trevor Harris chassis was used, it was miles better than the previous Lola design."

Don Devendorf: "The 1988 car had twice the downforce of the original Lola T810 with the same amount of drag. We could now use softer springing as the car was more compliant in every way, particularly over the bumps that you find at street circuits. That was a huge advantage over the opposition."

Goodyear tires replaced the Bridgestones previously used, as Bridgestone refused to sign a new contract with Electramotive, which stated that Bridgestone would pay for car damage that was a result of a tire blowout.

Ashley Page: "Of course, we were continually developing the car and nobody anticipated the downforce that it produced. The Bridgestone tires were woefully inadequate. When we changed to Goodyears, we were immediately two seconds faster per lap than with the Bridgestones. The Bridgestone people bought Japanese engineers to Portland who brought strain gauges to measure the downforce. When they saw what the gauges read, they wouldn't support the team anymore."

"Don Devendorf always did things his way, so we had better gears than anyone else. Everything was pretty special. The original engine's cast iron block would last five to six hours and then you would throw it away. Casting the block in aluminum solved that problem. 'Course, they were always production cylinder heads that we used."

"By 1988, the new bodywork was getting easier to work on. We had the new, Trevor Harris-designed tub, we built all the suspension pieces and bellhousing in house. The car had little to do with Lola by 1987. Everything was fabricated in house. There was a great electronics department with six electronics guys working in it. Almost all the Nissan stuff was made in Los Angeles."

"I'll always believe one of the reasons that we finally made it win was that we made the car easier to work on. Devendorf developed his own data acquisition system and the telemetry was a huge asset. He's someone that I thoroughly enjoyed working for. John Knepp had a lot to do with the initial engine development."

"By 1988, there were two factors that made us winners: The same group of people who'd seen this through from the get-go in 1984-5 were still there; Geoff Brabham was absolutely professional, better than anyone, in my opinion and Trevor (Harris) and Don (Devendorf) were great people and we reached that level where if you made a mistake you could clean it up."

"Those Electramotive turbochargers (Air Research) and waste-gates (manufactured at Electramotive) and, more importantly, the control system were some of the most sophisticated of their day. And the fabrication on them was top notch. We took a lot of weight out of the turbochargers as well. There was a lot of experimentation with different wheels on both the hot and cold side. The Air Research facility was also in El Segundo and those people had a very high interest in what was going on. It was very interesting."

Geoff Brabham: "I stopped Indycar racing at the end of 1987 and, coincidentally, we started winning with the Nissan in 1988. We won so many races, but it wasn't easy. There were some very hard battles. Don't forget that we were racing against the TWR Jaguars and Corvettes – they were very fast. We had a great rivalry with the Jaguars."

"That 1988 Nissan GTP ZX was very good through medium speed bends. We had races where the Jaguars were better suited to the track but the Nissan had very good traction. We had some great races. Don't forget that the 1988 rules played into Nissan's hands. The Goodyear tires were heaps better than the Bridgestones and we were using a thousand revs less than before. That gave us reliability and more low-down torque to help the car get out of the corners."

Nissan dominated IMSA racing in 1988, much to the dismay of the newly-arrived TWR Jaguars. Don Devendorf: "The TWR boys had seen that we were fast, but that the car never finished a race before 1988. That made them really happy."

Knowing that their strength lay in the shorter, sprint races, Electramotive avoided the early races at Daytona and Sebring, but after that, Geoff Brabham, using the new chassis '8801', won almost every race in the 1988 season, taking nine wins (including eight in a row), usually partnered by John Morton. Nissan lost the manufacturers' title to Porsche by just one point in 1988 (Porsche had strength in numbers with the privateer's 962's), but Geoff Brabham became the IMSA GTP Drivers' Champion.

Trevor Harris: "In 1988, when we

Nissan: The GTP & Group C Racecars 1984-1993

Even at night, testing went on. [Photo: Courtesy of Ashley Page.]

started out the season, Kas thought we would run a few selected races. He had only a little budget; there was a question mark about Nissan carrying on financing the GTP effort."

"It was very clear by Miami that we had an extremely competitive car. Geoff took the pole and led all the way until dropping out. It was planned to run the next eight races. But the way it worked, once we started winning, we couldn't stop! Nissan and Kas were forced to carry on. Geoff Brabham and John Morton won just about everything in sight. As it turned out, the car was very forgiving; very good to work on. The engine always ran with Don's injection. He did a terrific job with it."

In 1989, Brabham and new signing Chip Robinson bettered even the previous year's record with ten wins between them, including the Sebring 12 Hours with assistance from Arie Luyendyk. The only serious opposition for Brabham's second title came from Robinson, when they were in different cars. At the season's end Robinson was a close second in points and Nissan now claimed the Makes Title, at last.

Geoff Brabham: "Don't forget that at this time, we also had a great team. If we were pushed backwards at any race, we

In 1988 and 1989, this was the usual pose for the Electramotive team. At Portland, at GI Joe's Grand Prix, they posted yet another win. [Photo: Courtesy of Ashley Page.]

could simply come back the next weekend and win, just because of how good the team was."

John Morton: "I started racing with Nissans back in 1969 with roadsters and then with 510s. In 1987, I was driving the Jaguar XJRs for Bob Tullius and my teammate was Hurley Haywood. He was driving the Electramotive Nissans when Geoff Brabham was fulfilling his other driving commitments."

"Hurley, for some reason, didn't like the Nissans (Hurley Haywood: "I liked the car, I just didn't like the way the Bridgestones failed!") and so, at Sears Point in 1987, he left the team and I got his job. At the end of the season, Elliott, (Forbes-Robinson), also quit because he didn't like the tires, they blew out too often for his liking!"

"There were really, in my opinion, two major factors why the Electramotive Nissans were so dominant in 1988. Number one was tires. The switch over to Goodyears gave us more than a second a lap improvement straight away. The second thing was that IMSA hit us with restrictor plates. This kept the revs down and the engines, not being so highly stressed as before, became extremely reliable. If Don (Devendorf), could have had 1,000 horsepower, he would have gone after it. With the restrictors, we still had 750 horsepower. Plus a good 600 pounds foot of torque. The iron block of the "old" engine had failed when we used too much boost but now Electramotive developed the aluminum block, both lighter and stronger than the old iron one."

"You have to remember that not only was the car spectacular in every way, Electramotive was a very good team. The cars had incredible downforce but a lot of drag. Considering the horsepower available, they weren't that fast on the straight."

A second Chapman chassis '8802' had been built and delivered to Electramotive in 1988. This had been written off in testing at Lime Rock, with John Morton at the wheel, when it "flew" over the hill and so '8803' had been hurriedly built-up to replace it. The opposition was in disarray, as Porsche were now fading from the scene with the 962, Jaguar were developing their new XJR-10 V6 turbo and Dan Gurney's Eagle Toyotas were still on the learning curve. Nissan and Brabham were champions again.

ELECTRAMOTIVE NISSANS: 1985–1989 RACE RECORDS

LOLA T810:

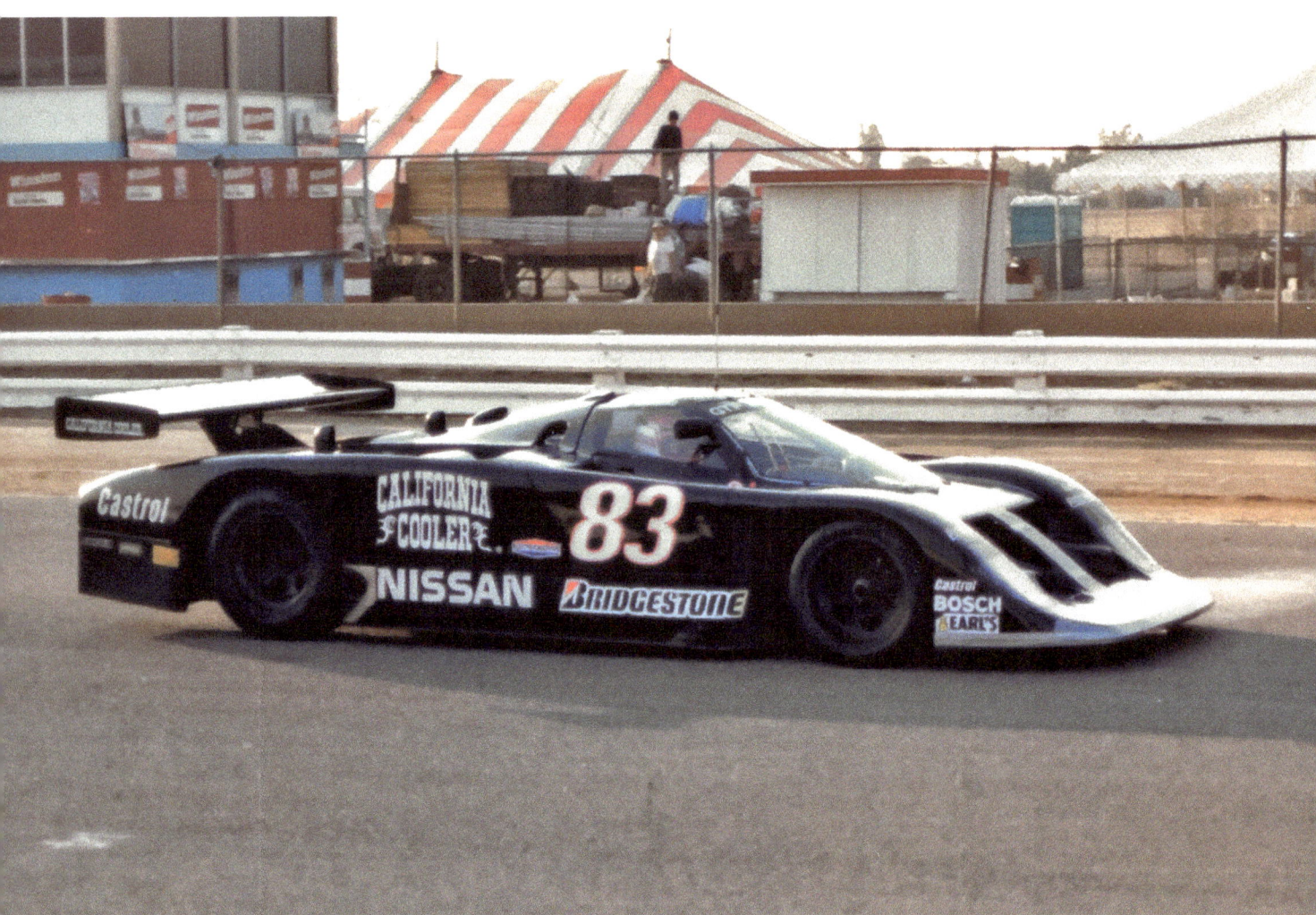

The Nissan GTP ZX Turbo (formerly Lola T810). [Photo: Courtesy of Ashley Page.]

A word about chassis histories

Ah, the chassis histories. We're living in an age where the "anoraks" (people who are anally retentive about this stuff) argue endlessly about which car did what, where.

Get a life, guys. I admit it – I'm one of you, and I've been doing this stuff for over twenty years now, but still mysteries abound. Where Nissans are concerned, they still do. Racing cars being what they are, cars get wrecked and sometimes, they re-appear under mysterious circumstances!

For instance, the Lola factory say that they only sold two T810s to Electramotive, in 1985. Trouble is, Nissan North American records show that 8701 "Elvis" was built on a Lola T810 chassis delivered in January 1987. Terry Nichols, the engineer who built up this car, says that he built it on: "An old Lola chassis that was lying around the works." There is also an 8702, built on a Lola chassis in existence today. At first, I thought that Electramotive must have bought the two T810s that were delivered to Japan, but Don Devendorf says emphatically, no, Electramotive did not buy the Japanese T810's. I can't square that circle.

Where 8801 and 8803 are concerned, there are more problems. Of course, 8801 was the first of the Trevor Harris designed Electramotive Nissans and this singleton car ran from the beginning of the 1988 season until July, when it was joined by 8803. (8802 was destroyed whilst testing at Lime Rock.) Nissan have issued me with a history of 8804, showing that car coming into the team in August 1989, doing a few races that year and some in the beginning of the 1990 season. 8805 was built up at NPTI when the team had already decided to use the NPTI90s and so never raced in period.

It would be easy to divide up the race numbers 83 and 84, assume that 8801 was always number 83 and appropriate the race results thusly. I've done this in the database, with one exception. Kas Kastner told me that the team would switch cars, (doors and front to change the race numbers) if, for instance, there was a problem with the designated racecar on race morning. He remembers that this definitely happened at Watkins Glen in 1988.

Then there are the NPTI90s. 90-02 and 04 were both written off over the infamous 1992 Road Atlanta weekend, one in practice, one in the race. Parts to build up several more cars were already fabricated when NPTI closed its doors and Louis Buffalo of Matrix Motors bought most of this and has and is building up new cars. To Louis' eternal credit, he is an enthusiast at heart and just wants to see more of these great cars out there.

In their day, there were never more than two cars at a time "out there" racing, sometimes with a spare, "back up" car in the trailer, just in case! And "just in case" happened a few times, which is why sometimes a car disappeared for a while, usually to re-appear a few weeks later, repaired and ready again for the track. Some didn't, as in the case of 8802, which was destroyed when John Morton was driving it at Lime Rock after just fifteen laps. Part of that car went into building up 8805.

Today, 8801, the Nissan with the greatest race history of all of them, still belongs to Nissan. 8803 was sadly badly damaged in the crash that took Bob Akin's life, but has been rebuilt. 8804 has happily always been in sight and 8805, despite being built up by NPTI after the '88 car's days were over, is still happily with the late Toby Bean's family.

HU-810/01
GTP ZX-T. Electramotive. Nissan V6 Turbo.

Difficult, now, to sort out the race records of HU-810/01 and /02. What is certain is that both cars were delivered to Electramotive, and HU810/01 was crashed at Pocono and at Charlotte. HU810/02, the spare, back up car was pressed into service whilst the other was repaired.

1985:
- 28/4: Riverside: Devendorf, #83; practice only. Withdrawn.
- 05/5: Laguna Seca: D. Devendorf/T. Adamowicz, #83; 11th
- 19/5: Charlotte: D. Devendorf, #83; Accident in practice. Repaired.
- 28/7: Portland: D. Devendorf/T. Adamowicz, #83; 16th NR.
- 04/8: Sears Point: D. Devendorf/T. Adamowicz, #83; 9th.
- 25/8: Road America: D. Devendorf, #83; 43rd NR.
- 08/9: Pocono: D. Devendorf, #83; 40th NR. Acc.

Repaired, using new, un-numbered tub sent by Lola Cars Ltd. The original, crashed tub was stored at the Electramotive shop.

1986: New car re-numbered as Nissan 86.01.
- 02/3: Miami GP: E. Forbes-Robinson/T. Adamowicz, #83; 10th.
- 27/4: Riverside: G. Brabham/E. Forbes-Robinson, #83; DNF. (Accident.)
- 04/5: Laguna Seca: E. Forbes-Robinson, #83; DNF.
- 08/6: Mid-Ohio: E. Forbes-Robinson/L. Heimrath, Jr. #83;7th.
- 27/7: Portland: G. Brabham, #83; Pole, 3rd.
- 03/8: Sears Point: E. Forbes-Robinson, #83; 4th.
- 24/8: Road America: G. Brabham/E. Forbes-Robinson, #83; DNF.
- 21/9: Watkins Glen: J. Lammers/E. Forbes-Robinson, #83; 18th.
- 05/10: Columbus: E. Forbes-Robinson/G. Brabham, #83; 5th.

Sold to Matrix Motors.

2002: Sold to Benton Bryan.
2003: Sold to Jacob Shalit
2018: STPO.

HU-810/02
Electramotive. Nissan V6 Turbo. In 1986, re-numbered as Nissan 86.02. See notes on HU810/01.

1985:
06/10: Columbus: D. Devendorf/T. Adamowicz, #83; 13th NR.

1986: Re-numbered as Nissan 8602. Used as the spare/backup car at races.

1987: Used as the principal car.
01/3: Miami GP: G. Brabham/E. Forbes-Robinson; 1st. 86.02 scored Electramotive Nissan's first IMSA victory.
12/4: Atlanta: E. Forbes-Robinson/H. Haywood; 18th. (Clutch.)
26/4: Riverside: G. Brabham/E. Forbes-Robinson; 21st. (Tire – accident.)
03/5: Laguna Seca: D. Hobbs; 5th.
07/6: Mid-Ohio: G. Brabham/E. Forbes-Robinson; DNF. (Cracked cross-member.)
05/7: Watkins Glen: H. Haywood/E. Forbes-Robinson; DNF. (Tire.)

26/7: Portland: G. Brabham/E. Forbes-Robinson; DNF. (Overheating.)
02/8: Sears Point: J. Morton/E. Forbes-Robinson; 17th. (Oil pressure.)
16/8: Road America: J. Morton/E. Forbes-Robinson; 16th. (Coil.)
06/9: San Antonio: E. Forbes-Robinson; DNF. (Accident.)
04/10: Columbus: G. Brabham/E. Forbes-Robinson; 28th OA. (Diff.)
25/10: Del Mar: G. Brabham/E. Forbes-Robinson; 6th. (Spin.)

1988: Rebuilt with parts from 88-02.
28/2: Miami GP: G. Brabham/J. Morton; Qualified 6th. DNS. (Team used 88.01 in the race.)
11/4: Road Atlanta: G. Brabham; Qualified Pole. DNS. (Team used 88.01 in the race.)

Turned into a Show car.

2002: In New York.
2005: Sold to Lilo Beuzieron.
2008: STPO. In restoration.
2017: Still with Lilo Beuzieron.

HU-810/03: Sold to Japan.
Raced in All-Japan Sportscar series.
HU-810/04: Sold to Japan.
Raced in All-Japan Sportscar series.

2003: Sold.

8701:
Built up in 1989 by Terry Nichols of Electramotive on the old crashed chassis, (repaired by Dan Mason), of T810/01, 8701 was used a spare car for one or two races.
　　In 1990, she was sold to Jim Busby's team as a back up car and, at West Palm Beach, came second overall, to demonstrate how competitive the old design still was! Sold to Rene Herzog, 8701 did a few Interserie races and was then put into storage; In 2007 she was bought by the irrepressible Kent Abrahamson, who raced her enthusiastically in Group C races in Europe.

2016: Sold to Stefano Rosina as 8702.
2017: Still in Europe.

8801:
G. Brabham's 1988 IMSA GTP Championship winner.
　　8801 was the first Electramotive Nissan built up with the new, Trevor Harris-designed chassis, Hewland gearbox and electronic wastegate. Fitted with the IMSA-mandated 3.0 liter engine, it pulverized the opposition in 1988, winning "eight straight" victories and nine in total to give Geoff Brabham a well deserved IMSA Camel Championship. In 1989, it scored seven victories to give the championship to Brabham yet again.
Retired to make way for the new NPTI90, 8801 was retained by the factory at it's museum in Japan.

1988:
28/3: Miami GP: G. Brabham/J. Morton, #83; 8th.
10/4: Road Atlanta: G. Brabham, #3; 1st.
24/4: West Palm Beach: G. Brabham/J. Morton, #83; 1st.

NISSAN: THE GTP & GROUP C RACECARS 1984-1993

28/5: Lime Rock: G. Brabham, #83; 1st.
05/6: Mid-Ohio: G. Brabham/T. Gloy, #83; 1st.
03/7: Watkins Glen: G. Brabham/J. Morton, #83; 1st.
17/7: Road America: G. Brabham/J. Morton, #83; 1st.
31/7: Portland: G. Brabham, #83; 1st.
14/8: Sears Point: G. Brabham, #83; 1st.
04/9: San Antonio: G. Brabham/J. Morton, #83; 12th.
02/10: Columbus: G. Brabham, #83; 1st.
23/10: Del Mar: G. Brabham, #83; 22nd NR.
27/11: Tampa: G. Brabham/J. Morton, #83; 1st.

1989:
04/2: Daytona 24-Hours: G. Brabham/C. Robinson/A. Luyendyk/M. Roe, #83; 27th NR. (Engine.)
05/3: Miami GP: G. Brabham/C. Robinson, #83; 1st.
18/3: Sebring 12-Hours: G. Brabham/C. Robinson/A. Luyendyk, #83; 1st.
02/4: Road Atlanta: G. Brabham/C. Robinson, #83; 1st.
23/4: West Palm Beach: G. Brabham, #83; 21st NR. (Engine.)
29/5: Lime Rock: C. Robinson, #83; 4th.
04/6: Mid-Ohio: G. Brabham/C. Robinson, #83; 1st.
02/7: Watkins Glen: G. Brabham/C. Robinson, #83; DNS.
16/7: Road America: G. Brabham/C. Robinson, #83; 1st.
30/7: Portland: G. Brabham/C. Robinson, #83; 2nd.
13/8: Topeka: G. Brabham, #83; 1st.
03/9: San Antonio: G. Brabham, #83; 15th. (Engine.)
10/9: Sears Point: G. Brabham, #83; 1st.
01/10: Tampa: G. Brabham, #83; 6th.

1990:
03/2: Daytona 24-Hours: G. Brabham/C. Robinson/D. Daly, #83; 30th NR. (Engine.)
25/2: Miami GP: D. Daly/R. Earl, #83; 19th.
17/3: Sebring 12-Hours: D. Daly/R. Earl, #83; 1st.

01/4: Road Atlanta: G. Brabham/D. Daly, #83; 1st.
22/4: Palm Beach: G. Brabham/D. Daly, #83; 1st.

2002: On display at the Nissan Museum in Japan.
2003: On loan to the Petersen Museum, L.A.

8802:

8802 did not live long! At Lime Rock, with John Morton at the wheel, it "flew" whilst testing and was destroyed. Some parts were, apparently, used in the build of 8805.

1988:
27/5: Destroyed at Lime Rock when testing with John Morton driving after fifteen laps in testing. Parts were used for 8805.

2016: Perhaps sold?

8803:

8803 was the #84 car of late 1988 and 1989. It scored two victories in 1989 and was then sold to Jim Busby's team and mainly driven by John Paul, who scored some excellent results but could never quite match the works team of NPTI90s!

8803 passed through the hands of several notable vintage racers before being involved in the accident, which took the life of noted racer Bob Akin at Road Atlanta. Today, she has been returned to her former glory.

1988:
31/7: Portland: J. Morton, #84; 2nd.
14/8: Sears Point: J. Morton, #84; 6th.
02/10: Columbus: D. Daly, #84; 7th.
23/10: Del Mar: D. Daly, #84; 4th.

1989:
04/2-05/2: Daytona 24-Hours: M. Rowe, #84; 61st NR.
18/3: Sebring 12-Hours: C. Robinson, Arie Luyendyk, #84; 52nd NR.
23/4: Palm Beach: G. Brabham/C. Robinson, #84; 6th.
29/5: Lime Rock: G. Brabham, #84; 1st.
02/7: Watkins Glen: G. Brabham/C. Robinson, #84; 1st.
30/7: Portland: C. Robinson, #84; 3rd.
??/12: Sold to Jim Busby Racing.

1990:
03/2: Daytona 24-Hours: K. Cogan/J. Paul, Jr./M. Baldi, #67; 25th NR. (Engine.)
25/2: Miami GP: K. Cogan/J. Paul, Jr., #67; 2nd.
17/3: Sebring 12-Hours: K. Cogan/J. Paul, Jr., #67; 5th.

Team sold to David Seabrook.

22/4: Palm Beach: K. Cogan/J. Paul, Jr., #67; 5th.
06/5: Topeka: K. Cogan/J. Paul, Jr., #67; 7th.
28/5: Lime Rock: K. Cogan/J. Paul, Jr., #67; 13th.
03/6: Mid-Ohio: J. Paul, Jr., #67; 18th NR (Gearbox.)
01/7: Watkins Glen: J. Villeneuve/J. Paul, Jr., #67; 14th NR. (Engine.)
15/7: Sears Point: J. Paul, Jr./J. Villeneuve, #67; 7th.
29/7: Portland: J. Paul, Jr., #67; 5th.

NISSAN: THE GTP & GROUP C RACECARS 1984-1993

19/8: Road America: J. Paul, Jr., #67; 5th.
02/9: San Antonio: J. Paul, Jr., #67; 9th.
30/9: Tampa: J. Paul, Jr., #67; 3rd.
11/11: Del Mar: J. Paul, Jr., #67; 3rd.

1/1991: Sold to Maurice Shirazi.

11/1992: Sold to Bob Pond.

1998: Sold to Michael Lauer. Vintage raced.

2002: Sold to Wayne Jackson.
25/4: Crashed at Road Atlanta. Bob Akin, the driver, was tragically fatally injured in the accident.

2018: The car has been rebuilt.

8804:
8804 was the #84 team car of 1989 and mainly driven by Chip Robinson, who won at San Antonio and scored several other top three places. In 1989, 8804 won the Sebring 12 Hours.

1989:
13/8: Topeka: C. Robinson, #84; 2nd.
03/9: San Antonio: C. Robinson, #84; 1st.
10/9: Sears Point: C. Robinson, #84; 2nd.
01/10: Tampa: C. Robinson, #84; 4th.
22/10: Del Mar: C. Robinson, #84; 17th NR. (halfshaft).

Victory! The expected outcome of an IMSA Camel GT race during 1988 and 1989. The Nissan 300 ZX GTP Turbos were totally dominant and Geoff Brabham was virtually unstoppable on his way to two consecutive IMSA Drivers' Championships. [Photo: Courtesy of Ashley Page.]

20/12: Riverside: Goodyear tire test. G. Brabham, #84.

1990:
03/2: Daytona 24-Hours: C. Robinson/B. Earl, #84; 28th NR. Engine
25/2: Miami GP: G. Brabham/D. Daly, #84; 1st.
17/3: Sebring 12-Hours: D.Daly/B. Earl, #84;1st.
01/4: Road Atlanta: C. Robinson, #84; 22nd NR. (Engine.)
22/4: Palm Beach: C. Robinson/B. Earl, #1; DNS. (Acc. on Sat. Morning).
06/5: Topeka: C. Robinson/B. Earl #84; 2nd.
28/5: Lime Rock: C. Robinson/B. Earl, #84; 4th.
03/6: Mid Ohio: C. Robinson/B. Earl, #84; 2nd.
01/7: Watkins Glen: G. Brabham. #83; 5th.

7/1990: Sold to Maurice Shirazi.

8/1995: Sold at Monterey auction.

25/4/1996: STPO.

2002: In Wisconsin.

8805:
Built up to replace 8802 after the fact, 8805 appears to have been a test and development car for the team.

1990: Used as a test car.

1995:
28/03: Sold to Jack Dunn.

1997:
??/10: Sold to Benton Bryan.
??/12: Sold to Toby Bean. Vintage raced.

2018: With Theodore Bean, USA.

Nissan Electramotive GTP/Lola T810 (1985)

Chassis	Monocoque in aluminum, built by Lola Cars Ltd, England. Designed by Eric Broadley.
Bodywork	Carbon Fiber and Kevlar.
Engine	Nissan VG30 GTP V6 at 60 degrees, supplied by Electramotive Engineering, USA. Two valves per cylinder. 1 x Garrett turbocharger TO3.
Compression Ratio	8.5:1.
Bore and Stroke	87 x 83 mm.
Capacity	2958.9 cc.
Power	Up to 1000 bhp @ 7600 rpm.
Torque	70 mkg @ 5600 rpm.
Electronic Engine Management	Don Devendorf designed electronic.
Gearbox	Weisman with 5 forward, 1 reverse gears.
Weight	850 kg.
Wheelbase	2705 mm.
Length	4800 mm.
Width	1990 mm.
Height	1070 mm.
Tires	Bridgestone.
Wheels	BBS: 11 x 16 fronts, 14 x 16 rears.
Brakes	AP.

Nissan GTP 300ZX-Turbo

Entrant	Nissan Performance Technology, Inc. 2652 La Mirada Drive Vista, Calif. 92083
Engine	Nissan turbocharged V-6, single overhead cam, aluminum heads, aluminum block. Garrett AIResearch turbo.
Fuel Injection	Nissan Performance Technology-prepared engine control processor designed by Don Devendorf.
Chassis	Aluminum honeycomb "tub."
Suspension	Front and rear suspension featuring individual unequal length A-arms and coil springs with adjustable shock absorbers. Rear outboard shock absorbers.
Transmission	Hewland VG-C, 5-speed transaxle.
Weight	2150 pounds.
Height	40 inches.
Width	79 inches.
Length	189 inches.
Wheelbase	106.5 inches.
Fuel Capacity	31.7 gallons.
Brakes	Four-wheel disc with AP six-piston calipers.
Wheels	(F) BBS Modular 13.0 x 17.0. (R) BBS Modular 15.0 x 17.0.
Tires	(F) Goodyear Radials 25.5 x 12.5 x 17.0. (R) Goodyear Radials 28.0 x 14.5 x 17.0.
Drivers	Geoff Brabham, Manalapan, Fla. Chip Robinson, Jacksonville, Fla. Derek Daly, Noblesville, In. Bob Earl, Larkspur, Ca.

1990 NPTI

2

NPTI 9003 at Mid-Ohio in 1991. [Photo: Courtesy of Daniel Mainzer.]

By 1990, Don Devendorf's team had been reorganized and retitled "Nissan Performance Technology, Inc." (NPTI). This was now a wholly owned subsidiary of Nissan USA. John Knepp refused to sell Electramotive Inc., and the new headquarters of NPTI moved to Vista, still in California. John Knepp: "When I saw the growth of NPTI, from our little core of about seven people to over two hundred, I could see that the company was headed for trouble and opted out."

"The 1990 car was not as good as the '88 car had been. The decision to go twin-turbo was, in my opinion, wrong. The new twin-cam heads were 70 pounds heavier and it was not a good cylinder head design."

Someone else who left Electramotive at this time was Yoshi Suzuka: "I left Electramotive and returned to work for Nissan in Japan in 1989. I had already designed the new car, but the NPTI management kept on changing things on it without testing the changes."

The Trevor Harris design of 1988 went on winning in the early part of 1990, scoring a 1-2 at Sebring and a clutch of other victories, before it was replaced by a new model at Mid-Ohio, where it scored victory, straight out of the box, so to speak.

Trevor Harris had designed the chassis of this new Nissan, the NPTI-90, which featured a front-mounted radiator with lower bodywork than the previous car and a short tail with a huge wing hung off the back. The engine air intake was now transferred to the roof.

Trevor Harris: "We could have carried on developing the 1988 car and it could have been as good as the NPTI-90."

"That car was different because of the aerodynamics. The body was designed first in the wind tunnel. I had decided that this was the way to go and that I would do a chassis to fit it afterwards. The NPTI 90's bodywork developed a lot more downforce than the 88 car's. It also came with some drag reduction, and that looked as if it would be a big plus."

"What was difficult was that the radiator was in the back of the car and I had to get air from the front intake to the rear. I flowed the air through a large tube, with an odd shape, that ran the length of the car. The suspension members went through the tube. This chassis was dimensionally totally different to the 88 car."

"The NPTI 90 finished up 80% stiffer (than the 88 car) because the cross-section of the monocoque was much larger. At the side, the pontoons were open with cross braces at the ends, which was a little bit unusual. The lower "A" arm went right through the duct. It was more complicated than the 88 car but more reliable."

John Morton: "I personally think that the 88 car, had it kept on being developed, would have been every bit as good as the

NPTI 9001. [Photo: Author's collection.]

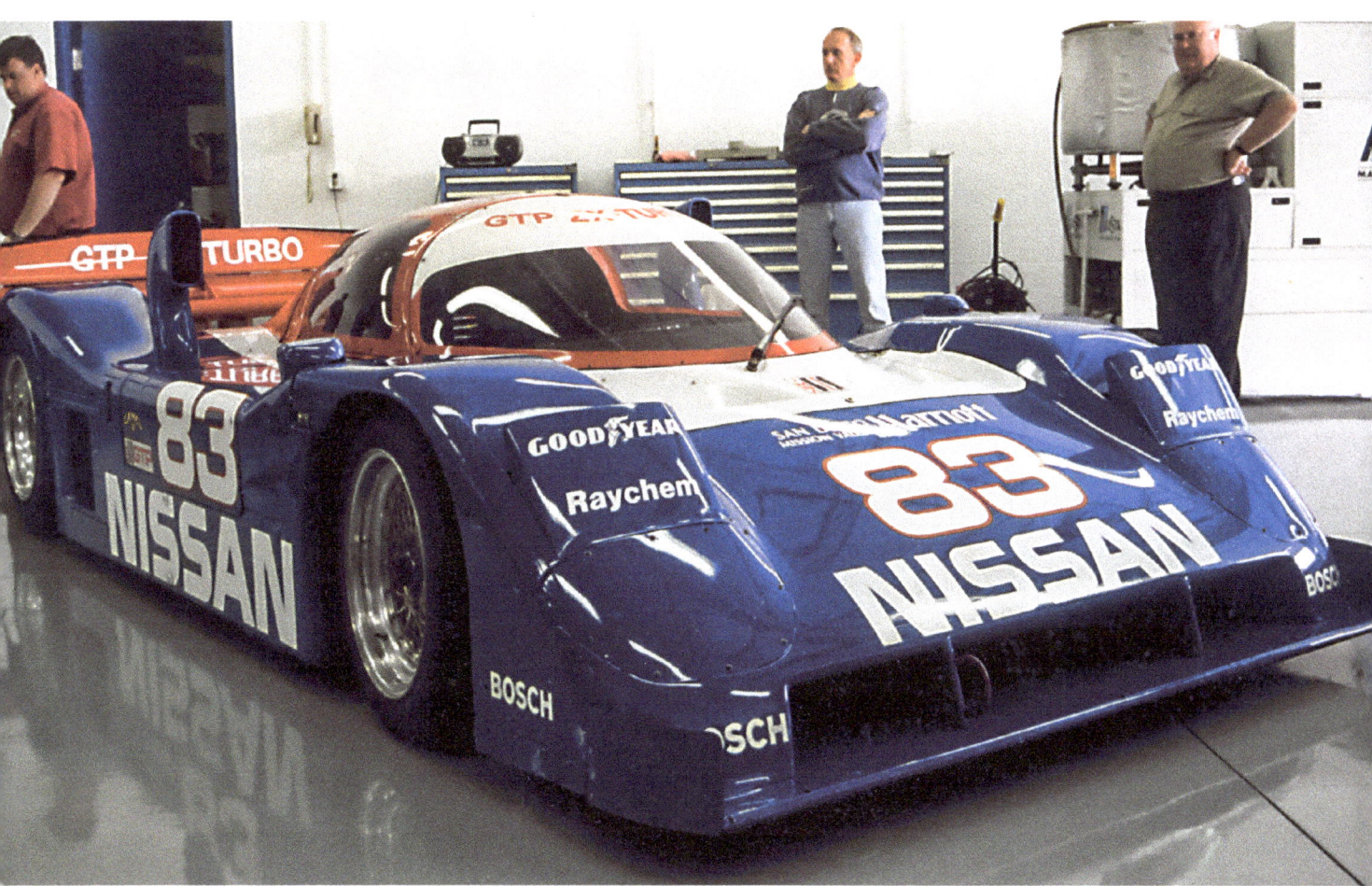

90 Nissan. I think that Nissan spent so much money on the NPTI-90, they just had to make it work. No matter which way you look at it though, they were spectacular, state of the art, racecars. Really, the best of the bunch."

At the end of the season, Brabham and Chip Robinson were first and second in the Drivers' Championship and Nissan had won the title yet again.

Don Devendorf: "I suppose that we could have carried on with the 1988 car, kept

The rear of NPTI9001. [Photo: Author's collection.]

on developing it, and it would have achieved the same results as the 1990 car did. But you have to remember that we were on top of the whole scene in 1989 and it seemed to make sense to bring out a new car."

Curt Geatches: "Of course, Electramotive/NPTI made the new engines in-house. They were reduced in capacity to 2.5-liters in order to take advantage of an IMSA-sanctioned rule, which gave us a better weight break. That four-valve V-6 needed sorting when it was first run. The oil pump was a bad copy of the English Cosworth pump and it was a disaster. It took a complete redesign to save it."

Don Williams: "The engines were very powerful. I still have a photo somewhere of John Knepp's dynamometer with a four-valve engine on test. It's showing over 1190 horsepower. 'Course, we never raced them producing that much power; that was for qualifying."

NISSAN: THE GTP & GROUP C RACECARS 1984-1993

Demonstrating just how good the older car was, it should be mentioned that, at the West Palm Beach race of April 22nd, 1990, Chip Robinson crashed his car during practice on Friday morning. Jim Busby had bought the old "Elvis" (8701) and used it as a back-up to 8803, which he had also bought from Electramotive. Busby loaned "Elvis" to NPTI and, after the mechanics had worked on it till 3.30. a.m., Robinson qualified it

For the first half of the 1990 season, whilst the new NPTI 90 was being thoroughly tested, the NPTI team stayed with the old 1988/89-style car. This is Geoff Brabham, partnered with Derek Daly, winning at Mid-Ohio in June. [Photo: Courtesy of Daniel Mainzer.]

The monocoque tub of the NPTI 90 under construction. [Photo: Courtesy of Ashley Page.]

eleventh on the grid later that day (Saturday). In the race, Robinson and Bob Earl finished second overall with it.

Jim Busby: "The Nissan was not so very different where the chassis and the brakes and steering were concerned to our old Porsche 962s that we'd been running – maybe just a little bit better. But when it came to the power – that was where things were on a different level. The electronic management was something else, I mean the NPTI boys would map the car with their computers for each circuit, not just change the chip as we had done with the Porsche."

"The Achilles heel of the Nissan

NISSAN: THE GTP & GROUP C RACECARS 1984-1993

In 1990 Jim Busby bought chassis number 8803 from NPTI and entrusted it to John Paul, Jr. and Kevin Cogan for the IMSA Camel GT season. They posted some good finishes, including a second at the Miami Grand Prix and a third at Del Mar. At Sears Point in July, John Paul, Jr. shared the driving with Jacques Villeneuve.
[Photos: Courtesy of Daniel Mainzer.]

two-valve engines that we ran was the cylinder heads. They were still Nissan stock items and would crack if pushed too far in a race. The trick was to let the engines develop full power for a couple of laps, but then turn the boost down to save them. 'Course, we only had a five million dollar a year budget, as against Nissan's twenty million a year and that put us into a different ballgame to NPTI, so we didn't have much luck."

"Also, the Nissan was an expensive car to maintain – it needed virtually every part renewed after every race, not like the Porsche, which was very sturdy and reliable. Still, you could see that, if everything lasted, winning races was like shooting fish in a barrel."

Geoff Brabham: "The 1990 car was not as good as the 1988 car had been at the outset. If our team had a deficiency, I think that it was in the wind tunnel. I don't think that the results that we got in the tunnel translated onto the track. In other words, the aero package was not as good as other teams, such as the Eagle Toyotas and the later TWR-Turbo Jaguars were."

John and Paul Reisman (Father and Son) own NPTI9007 today and race her enthusiastically in the HSR "Thundersports" series. Here is the car at Daytona in 2002. [Photo courtesy of Paul Reisman.]

"We were pulling a huge rear wing to get enough down-force, but that also created a lot of drag. A good ground effect car only needs a small wing. Thankfully, we had a very strong engine, so we could use the power to overcome the aerodynamic disadvantage. I think that if the '90 car's engine had been put in the 1988 car, that would have been as good, if not better. If you look at the results over the four years, 1988 to 1992, you can see that we were going backwards over the last two years."

At Daytona, at the beginning of 1991, NPTI ran a pair of "English" Lola–Nissan Group C R90C cars. Brabham, partnered by Earl, Robinson and Daly, finished second to the TWR Jaguar but Sebring saw a victory. New, twenty-four valve engines powered the NPT-91 at Road Atlanta and Chip Robinson placed second here and then won at Topeka and Lime Rock. Just one month after its first race, the NPTI90 was driven to victory at Mid-Ohio in June, by Derek Daly and Geoff Brabham. In the final race at Del Mar, Brabham took the title yet again when he finished third and Robinson slumped to seventh.

The lightweight Eagle Toyotas were now showing themselves as the main threat even though Jaguar were providing slightly tougher opposition, but the ZX-Ts still dominated and both Nissan and Brabham kept their Championships.

In 1992, the Toyotas came good with their lightweight Eagles, even though Trevor Harris had pared two hundred pounds from the NPTI90. (In house, this was designated as the NPT-91C.) Still, it wasn't enough to beat Toyota. Miami was Nissan's only victory. Brabham finished the season in third place in the Drivers' Championship, Nissan were second in the Manufacturer's Championship.

Kas Kastner: "When we saw how successful the Toyota Eagle was, by going to the ultra-lightweight configuration that the IMSA rules allowed, we developed the basic design in a variety of ways. The 'A' was as the normal tested version and started the 1992 season and the 'D' (90-06) was equipped with a 2.5-liter engine with a single turbo and traction control. It was the lightest Nissan ever built at 1920 pounds. It was raced at Phoenix and Del Mar and then the car was returned to the 'C' configuration before sale. I don't remember some of them but I named them thus to keep the differences noted between the spare cars and the updated ones. I believe a 6 speed gearbox was one of the changes, and the side big air scoops was another."

"The racing in those years was both exciting and close. I remember that at Tampa, in 1990, Chip was leading and he and Geoff both pitted at the same time. Chip was slow moving out the pit lane and Geoff passed him in the pitlane before the exit to the track. The officials called me to see what was going on as apparently they didn't know what to do. I explained that the pitlane was part of the racing surface and, therefore, it was a legitimate pass. They said, 'Oh! Yeah, okay.' Fun stuff."

"There was big crash for Geoff at Del Mar also. You must remember I was on the radio to Donny (Crew Chief), the drivers, plus the pitlane and the pit board people so it got a little busy sometimes. I was taking the lap times and the intervals also and then scoring that in my notebook."

"The thing about it that is rather funny is that I had an ear plug in the right ear for the cars and pits and scoring and in the other ear another plug for the scanner to listen in to IMSA and all the other cars. Great stuff. Does the phrase "one armed paper hanger" mean anything to you?"

A new car was needed. Harris was instructed by Nissan in Japan to use their new, 3.5-liter V12 motor. Don Devendorf and Yoshi Suzuka designed a new body and Trevor Harris designed a new tub, two of which were built, one in aluminum honeycomb, and one in carbon-fiber/Kevlar composite.

Don Devendorf: "The V-6 had been a good engine that we had developed from scratch in seven months. The aluminum block that we made for that engine was three times stronger than the original steel block. The Japanese-designed V-12 was not such a good engine as the V-6. I remember that every year, the Japanese designers would come over to us to look at what we were doing engine-wise. I kept telling them that they needed to use titanium valves and exhaust headers, stuff that we'd been using way back in the straight six engines but they'd never listen."

"I was very proud of Electramotive. I remember that we decided to design and build traction control into the GTP car. I had approached Bosch about their system, but their charges were outrageous. I told the design group on Monday morning how to lay it out and do it and we had a car testing with the system within seven days. We then went testing again and optimized the whole set-up at Phoenix. That's how good Electramotive was. Geoff (Brabham) used the system at Del Mar, as that circuit was very slippery. He tried switching it off for one lap and nearly crashed!"

"If we had bought out the 2.5-liter car, Gurney's Toyotas wouldn't have known what was happening. It's such a shame that IMSA went down the wrong path and couldn't come up with the TV package that the series needed to keep going."

Behind the scenes, the World's financial problems of the early '90's made themselves felt. Nissan lost money for the first time in '92 and Tom Mignanelli was forced to resign as the head of Nissan USA in '93. His replacement had been in charge of Nissan in Britain and had axed Nissan Motorsports Europe. He was put in charge of Nissan USA and dropped the axe on NPTI.

Kas Kastner: "I had a warning from Japan in 1992 that things were going badly for Nissan. When the axe fell, it was no great surprise. It was a great period and I only had one real disappointment. At Le Mans in 1990, we were two laps up on the Jaguar and ahead on the fuel allocation when the fuel bladder in the car burst and put us out."

Kastner auctioned the remnants of NPTI and closed the facility. The staff had grown to 271 from Electramotive's 70+ in 1988.

Ashley Page: "In 1991, I was working on the Mazda 787 GTP project and Trevor Harris called me in Del Mar to say: 'Hey, I hear your program is being shut down.' I said: 'Really, I haven't heard anything about it.' A month later, we were told we were being shut down! Then I heard something and called Trevor: 'I hear your program is being shut down.' 'No,' said Trevor, 'We're okay.' One month later, the Nissan program was over!"

Trevor Harris: "I was surprised at the NPTI close, I didn't think it was going to happen. Tom Mignanelli was our primary supporter and he had a brain tumor. Japan's bosses squeezed him out. He regarded our budget as his thirteenth month of Nissan's advertising budget. I know that we spent forty million dollars in 1990, but that did include our new building."

"Many of the Japanese managers were at odds with the American racing effort. I think that there was a huge chasm between what the Japanese wanted and what we gave 'em. There was some kind of feeling that they'd done everything."

"Electramotive/NPTI was a really good group that was very effective, although it had became a monster by 1992. The efficiency per person was reduced."

"Had we gone on and produced Group C cars, as was envisioned, it might have made sense. As it turned out, in 1993, we knew that as a result of cutbacks, there would have to be a reduction in the spending."

"We thought that we were doing the only Nissan Group C effort in the early 90s but Nissan in Japan were doing one too. Kent in the UK asked why a group from Nissan Japan were asking for castings for our gearbox."

"The V12 engine? We never had the right from Nissan to put one on the dyno – we were saddled with the world's worst V12 Group C engine. It had no horsepower to speak of. James Weaver tested it at Daytona for us. He got out and announced: 'There's no power. The engine wants to make power but something's off with the timing.'"

"We looked at Indycars, looking at everything about them. We took a Group C V12 engine and put it in an ex-Andretti car that we bought from Carl Haas in 1990. I worked out a tube frame adaptation and that allowed us to get the V-12 in it. We took it to a test with Steve Millen. After he'd driven it, he climbed out and said: 'This doesn't produce as much power as an Indy lights car.'"

"My favorite memory? I guess winning four Championships in a row and knowing that the team did a really good job.

To win so many races makes me so happy."

Geoff Brabham: "I think, to sum up, that that particular period, 1988 to 1990, was the most enjoyable period of my racing career. I just happened to be in the right place at the right time. It was great to wake up in the morning, knowing that you had the chance to go out there and win."

Louis Buffalo of Matrix Motors bought most of the remaining Nissan GTP cars plus several damaged chassis. Over the years, he has put most of them back into commission where they form the backbone of the "Thundersports" HSR series today.

In 1993, Gianpiero Moretti, owner of the "Momo" steering wheel Company, partnered by Derek Bell and John Paul, Jr., shared Moretti's NPTI 90-03 and placed second at Sebring.

Kevin Doran is a crew chief/team manager and has won the Daytona 24-Hours no less than five times (1986, 87, 89, 98 and 2002). When David Seabrook bought the Jim Busby/BF Goodrich team after Sebring in 1990, he looked after the two Nissans (88-03 and 87-01), although only 88-03 was regularly raced. He remembered the 1988 car as being: "A great car. Strong chassis, mega downforce! We had John Paul Jr., Kevin Cogan and Jacques Villeneuve Sr. driving with good results all season long."

"In 1993, I ran NPTI90-03 for Gianpiero Moretti whose co-driver was Derek Bell. It was much the same as the 1988 car, a good customer car that did not need much maintenance. About the only troubles we had were with the turbochargers. They were a sophisticated ball bearing mainshaft design, more efficient than the previous brass bearing ones."

"The NPTI90 had pretty traditional set up and handling – it responded to chassis changes in the way that a good race car should. Of course, compared to the budget that the Toyota-Eagles had, we were running on a pittance, so our results were pretty good, I think."

It was the end of the great IMSA GTP era, and one that Nissan had dominated from 1988 through 1991.

NPTI 90/01:

1990:
- 06/5: Topeka: Daly/Earl, #83; 8th.
- 26/5: Lime Rock: Brabham/Daly, #83; DNF. (Engine).
- 03/6: Mid-Ohio: Brabham/Daly, #83; 1st.
- 15/7: Sears Point: Brabham/Daly, #83; 2nd.
- 28/7: Portland: Brabham, #83; DNF. (Stuck Throttle).
- 19/8: Road America: Brabham, #83; 1st.
- 02/9: San Antonio: Brabham, #83; 3rd.

1991:
- 03/3: West Palm Beach: Brabham, #83; 3rd.
- 16/3: Sebring 12-Hours: Brabham/Daly, #83; 1st.
- 16/6: New Orleans: Brabham, #83; 2nd.

02/6: Mid-Ohio: Brabham, #83; 5th.
30/6: Watkins Glen: Brabham, #83; 2nd.
21/7: Laguna Seca: Brabham, #83; 2nd.
28/7: Portland:Brabham, #83; 2nd.
25/8: Road America: Robinson, #1; 2nd.
13/10: Del Mar: Brabham, #83; 3rd.

1992: "92C" Model. NPTI 6-speed gearbox.
28/6: Watkins Glen: Brabham, #83; DNF. (engine).

1995: May 24: Sold to Oliver Kuttner.
2001: November 7: Sold.
2007: Sold to RM Motorsport.
2017: With Nissan Factory?

90/02:

1990:
01/7: Watkins Glen: Robinson/Earl, #84; 1st.
15/7: Sears Point: Robinson, #84; 3rd.
28/7: Portland: Robinson, #84; 4th.
19/8: Road America: Robinson, #84; DNF.
02/9: San Antonio: C. Robinson, #84; 2nd.
30/9: Tampa: Robinson, #84; 2nd.
11/11: Del Mar: Robinson, #84; 5th.

1991:
03/3: West Palm Beach: Robinson, #84; DNF.
16/3: Sebring 12-Hours: Robinson/Earl, #84; 2nd.
07/4: Mimai GP: C. Robinson, #84; 5th.
28/4: Road Atlanta: Robinson, #84; 2nd.
05/5: Heartland: Robinson, #84; 1st.
27/5: Lime Rock: Robinson, #84; 1st.
02/6: Mid-Ohio: Robinson, #84; 6th.
16/6: New Orleans: Brabham, #83; 2nd.
30/6: Watkins Glen: Robinson, #84; 3rd.

25/8: Road America: Daly, #83; DNF.

1992: "92C" model.
28/4: Road Atlanta: Robinson, #84; DNF. (Crash).
Badly damaged. Re-Tubbed.

2017: Still in USA.

90/03:

1990:
02/9: San Antonio: Spare car, #1, did not race.
30/9: Tampa: Brabham, #83; DNF. (Acc).
11/11: Del Mar: Brabham, #83; 4th.

1991:
07/4: Miami: Brabham, #83; 3rd.
27/5: Lime Rock: Brabham, #83; 3rd.
16/6: New Orleans: Robinson, #84; 6th.
21/7: Laguna Seca: Robinson, #84; 5th.
28/7: Portland: Robinson, #84; 4th.
25/8: Road America: Earl, #84; 5th.
13/10: Del Mar: Robinson, #84; DNF. (Diff.).

Geoff Brabham then had a serious accident in testing at Road America. A new car was built up around a new tub.

1992: "92C" model. Hewland 5-speed g/box.
23/2: Miami: C. Robinson/B. Earl, #84; 3rd.
15/3: Sebring 12-Hours: Robinson/Earl/Luyendyk, #84; 2nd.
25/5: Lime Rock: Brabham, #83; 2nd.
31/5: Mid-Ohio: Brabham, #83; 3rd.
14/6: New Orleans: Brabham, #83; 2nd.
19/7: Laguna Seca: Brabham, #83; DNF. (Engine).

26/7: Portland: Brabham, #83; 6th.

1993: Leased to MOMO. Back up car. red/yellow. Crystal Wine Coolers sponsored.
23/2: Miami GP: M. Sigala; DNF. Returned to NPTI.

1995: Sold to O. Kuttner.
2002: Completely restored by Kevin Doran.
2007: Sold to U.K. (Phil Stott).

NOTE: The bent tub of the crashed car from the testing accident was repaired and another car built up around it by Matrix Motors, who had bought the rights from NPTI when that establishment closed down in 1993.

90/04: First car with the 4-valve headed engines. Six-speed gearbox. Lighter weight.

1991: NPT-91.
30/2: Daytona 24 Hours: G. Brabham/C. Robinson/D. Daly/B. Earl, #83X; 2nd.
28/4: Road Atlanta: Brabham, #83; DNF.
05/5: Heartlands: Daly; 5th.
04/7: Daytona: G. Brabham/D. Daly, #83; 3rd.
25/8: Road America, #83; DNS. Crash in practice.

Later on Re-Tubbed and rebuilt by Matrix Motors.

2018: STPO. Still in USA.

90/05: 4-valve engine, Lighter weight than first three cars.
1992: "83B" spec.
23/2: Miami: G. Brabham, #83; 1st.
21/3: Sebring 12-Hours: G. Brabham/D. Daly/A. Luyendyk/D. Brabham, #83; 2nd.
28/4: Road Atlanta: G. Brabham, #83; DNF. (Crash).

Repaired, using new chassis supplied by JC Prototypes, who supplied all the chassis panels for the original cars.

1993: Leased to Gianpiero Moretti, MOMO Team.

31/1: Daytona 24-Hours: Moretti/Bell; 3rd. (Led in the 20th hour-DNF by engine failure).
21/2: Miami: Moretti/Bell; 4th.
20/3: Sebring 12-Hours: Moretti/Bell, #30; 2nd.
18/4: Road Atlanta: Moretti/Bell, #30; 7th.
31/5: Lime Rock: Moretti/Bell, #30; 5th.
02/6: Mid-Ohio: Moretti/Bell, #30; 3rd.
30/6: Watkins Glen: Moretti/Bell, #30; 4th.
21/7: Laguna Seca: Bell, #30; 4th.
28/7: Portland: Moretti/Bell, #30; 4th.
25/8: Road America: Bell, #30; 4th.
13/10: Phoenix: Moretti/Bell, #30; 7th.

Hewland 5-speed g/box fitted.

1994:
Sold to Dr Jack Dunn, a surgeon from Texas. Repossessed by the Commerce Bank of Texas. Sold to Benton Bryan, (John Daniels Racing – he had two NPTI90s-2004: Le Mans support race with the other), by Joe Tobin. First car sold.

2000: Sold to John Reisman.
2006: Sold through John Starkey to present owner.
2018: Still in USA.

90/06:

1992: Light Blue. 2.5 liter engine, single turbo engine.
19/7: Laguna Seca: C. Robinson, #84; 3rd. (84-C)
26/7: Portland: C. Robinson, #84; 3rd. (84C)

1994: Brought up to 92C spec. Hewland 5-speed g/box.

1995: Sold to Bruce Canepa, USA.

90/07: Last car built and raced in period. 92C lightweight spec. Built in late 1991/early 1992.

1992: 2.5 liter single turbo engine. 1900 pounds.
04/10: Phoenix: G. Brabham, #83; 3rd. (83-D).
11/10: Del Mar: G. Brabham, #83; 2nd. (83-D).

1994: NPTI 6-speed g/box.

1999: Vintage raced by Brian de Vries.

90/08: Built by Matrix Motors.
Sold to Paul Wesserlink, USA.

90/09: Built by Matrix Motors.
Sold to Hudson Historics- Raced by Bob Akin.
Sold to Nigel James, UK.
Sold again.

90/10:
Built by Matrix Motors.
Sold to Peter Stoneberg.
2008: Sold to Don Coaster, UK.
2017: With Phil Stott. UK.

90/11: Built by Matrix Motors.
Sold to Jim Oppenheimer.
Sold to RM Motorsports. The black car.

2008: Sold to Kobsak Chinawongwatana.

90/12: Built by Matrix Motors.

2010: Sold to Chris and Nick Randall, UK.
2017: MOMO colors, Chris Randall.

90/14:
2010: Built by Matrix Motors.
Sold to Nick and Chris Randall, UK.

2017: NPTI colors. Still with the Randalls, UK.

90/15: Built by Matrix Motors.
Sold to Benton Bryan, USA.

90/16: Built by Matrix Motors.
Sold to Oliver Kuttner.

NOTE: There were 20 sets of panels supplied to build up chassis to NPTI. 4 cars were re-tubbed, hence total production of NPTI90s, both in period by NPTI, and afterwards as continuation cars by Matrix Motors, is 16, plus one crashed tub repaired and car built up around it.

Nissan GTP ZX-Turbo (NPTI91C)

Entrant	Nissan Performance Technology, Inc. 2641 La Mirada Drive Vista, Calif. 92083
Engine	Nissan twin-turbocharged 2.5-liter V-6, dual overhead cam, aluminum heads, aluminum block. Garrett AIResearch twin turbos.
Fuel Injection	Nissan Performance Technology-prepared electronic engine control processor designed by Don Devendorf.
Chassis	Aluminum honeycomb "tub."
Suspension	Front suspension featuring individual unequal length A-arms and coil springs operated by top-rocker with adjustable shock absorbers. Rear outboard shock absorbers.
Transmission	Hewland VG-C, 6-speed transaxle.
Height	40 inches.
Width	79 inches.
Length	189 inches.
Weight	1925 pounds.
Wheelbase	107.5 inches.
Fuel Capacity	31.7 gallons.
Brakes	Four-wheel disc, six-piston calipers.
Wheels	(F) BBS 13.0 x 17.0. (R) BBS 15.0 x 18.0.
Tires	(F) Goodyear Radials 25.5 x 12.0 x 17.0. (R) Goodyear Radials 29.5 x 16.5 x 18.0.
Drivers	Geoff Brabham, Manalapan, Fla. Chip Robinson, Jacksonville, Fla. Bob Earl, Purcellville, Va.

THE EUROPEAN
Group C Nissans

3

Hoshino and Hagiwara shared the driving of this March 83G in the Suzuka 500 Kilometer race of 1985. They qualified in fifth place and that's where they finished when the race ended. [Photo: Courtesy of Nissan.]

In 1985, Nissan of Japan decided to try and win Le Mans. As a start, they contracted with March Engineering of Bicester to build chassis for them based upon March's "Customer" 85G. This car had attempted to build upon the reputation of the successful March 82, 83 and 84Gs in IMSA GTP racing in America but, with the coming of the Porsche 962 in 1985, the March chassis was seen to be outclassed by that of the Porsche.

Nevertheless, in Japan, three 85Gs were entered for the Fuji 1000 km and Hoshino put his car on pole position on the first day of practice

Don Reynolds, who had built the engine for the March-Nissan, remembered: "I was in the restaurant at the circuit, talking with Derek Bell and Hans Stuck. Derek had just put the Porsche on pole before Hoshino out-did him. Derek was amazed at how fast the March-Nissan was. He reckoned that he'd got every corner just right, but: 'Hoshino went by me like a rocket. What's in that thing?' 'Course, the Japanese cheated like mad with rocket fuel, but that's another story!"

Porsche responded on the second practice day, pushing the March back on to the second row but race day dawned with a monsoon howling. All the European-entered cars withdrew and Hoshino led the Japanese contingent to outright victory, despite a spin halfway through the race.

In 1986, partly due to this success, Nissan purchased four March 86Gs. This was an all-new car, designed by Gordon Coppuck and called the 86S (Sport). For this car, Indycar type suspension was used, the tub being made out of aluminum honeycomb with magnesium bulkheads. It was narrower and lighter (by 100 kg) than the previous 85G cars with side-mounted radiators. Bodywork was in carbon-fiber and Kevlar. The Electramotive-built Nissan six-cylinder engine installed was the FB30 V6.

Co-incidentally BMW USA bought six 86G cars, to be engined with BMW's 2.5-liter four cylinder turbocharged engine. This 86G was, however, more akin to the earlier 85G as Gordon Coppuck had taken over at March in time to design the Japanese

Masahiro Hasemi and Takeo Wada drove this March 85G with a turbocharged VG30 engine installed at the Fuji 500 mile race of 1985. [Photo: Courtesy of Nissan.]

"Nissan" 86Gs, a completely separate design. Only the tub was the same as that of the BMW car. This "86G" is sometimes referred to as the "86S" to denote the difference between the two sets of 86Gs. Confusing, isn't it?

David Hobbs, BMW's chief driver in America, called their 86Gs: "unbelievably competitive" and thought that they would still have been competitive in 1989 had BMW North America put their full weight behind it. A look at the success of Electramotive's Nissans would seem to bear out this contention!

In 1986 the Marches were very fast in IMSA-sanctioned races, and victory

Hoshino and Nakago put this car on the pole at the Suzuka 1000 kilometer race in 1986. Sadly, the car was forced into retirement during the race. [Photo: Courtesy of Nissan.]

eluded them due to minor problems only. Sadly, at the end of the year, BMW stopped the program and that was that. Gianpiero Moretti bought two cars at the end of the season and equipped them with Buick engines, one a normally aspirated V-8 and one a turbo V-6. He and John Andretti raced them with little success until 1988.

When raced by Nissan, the 86S/G was known as the R86V and its engine, developed in conjunction with Electramotive, delivered over 1000 bhp on full boost. The motor used twin overhead camshafts with two valves per cylinder and had many parts made of titanium. Bosch fuel injectors were employed, in conjunction with Nissan EECP 16 bit microprocessors in the Electramotive engine management system. Race power was quoted as 700 horsepower at 8000 rpm.

Le Mans, 1986. Masahiro Hasemi, James Weaver and Takeo Wada drove a solid race in this Nissan-March 85G to finish in sixteenth place. Keith Greene, Nissan's team manager, believed that they should have been much higher up the finishing order, but management dictated a slow and steady pace to be sure of finishing. [Photo: Courtesy of Nissan.]

James Weaver stands in front of the Nissan R85V that he shared with Hasemi and Wada to place sixteenth at Le Mans in 1986. [Photo: Courtesy of Nissan.]

The decision was taken by NISMO (Nissan Motorsports) to enter Le Mans with an 86G and an older 85G and Keith Greene, who had been impressed by Hoshino's performance at Fuji, was nominated as Team Manager of the English-based Nissan Motorsport Europe (NME) to head up the operation.

The first 86G, after a fire whilst testing in Japan, was flown back to Bicester

The Nissan R85V in the pits at Le Mans in 1986
[Photo: Courtesy of Nissan.]

for repairs. Two weeks later, Keith Greene and the Nissan team took the car to Donington where, with James Weaver driving, the 86G performed much better than expected. Indeed, the team now saw that pole position at Le Mans was a possibility, despite the fact that Greene had provided a very special fuel for the Donington test. James Weaver reported driving the 86G as: "Picking the gears as fast as I could without looking at the rev counter."

Although possessing a very 'peaky' engine, the Nissan was fifth fastest at the Le Mans test days, despite teething troubles. Unfortunately, without the 'Jungle Juice' that the car had previously used, the engine misfired.

Sadly, a clash of cultures took place at Le Mans, the Japanese drivers having been told by their management to go slowly as the engine department had advised the management that the engines would not last

Nissan: The GTP & Group C Racecars 1984-1993

At Suzuka in the 1000 kilometer race of 1986, this March 86G, powered by the VG30 V6 engine, was driven by Matsumoto and Suzuki. [Photo: Courtesy of Nissan.]

if used hard. In vain, Greene ordered the drivers to go faster in practice, but was studiously ignored. The 86S's engine failed in the eighth hour, whilst the 85G finished, albeit in 16th place. Nissan were delighted that one of their cars had finished the race on their first try, whilst the English team personnel were disgusted at what they saw as a missed opportunity.

Don Reynolds, Electramotive's engine builder, remembered: "I built the first twin-cam engines for those cars. I must have built about twenty iron-block engines for those Le Mans cars. One of my engines was in the March-Nissan that finished at Le Mans. Afterwards, when we got that engine back and I stripped it, I saw that the rings were all worn out. The team hadn't run air cleaners and it had completely ruined those rings, leaving them with no compression. That's why the engines were so hard to start after the pitstops later in the race."

1987 saw March build just three cars for Nissan, these accommodating the new three-liter VEJ30 V8 engine. This had a bore and stroke of 85 x 66 mm. This engine had four gear driven overhead camshafts, and four valves per cylinder and two IHI turbochargers. Power was quoted as 700 bhp at 0.8 bar boost at 8,000 rpm.

The car itself had been designed by Paul Bentley and had an aluminum honeycomb monocoque chassis with magnesium bulkheads and uprights reinforced by upper carbon fiber panels. The radiators were side-mounted. The engine was mounted semi-stressed. New, lower bodywork was developed by Nick Wirth.

In the Le Mans 24-Hours, both cars were put out by engine failure. The older 86G had been sold to Tom Hanewa and was entered at Le Mans by the Italya Sports Team. It was faster at the test weekend than the newer cars, sporting an updated Electramotive engine. During qualifying for the race, the 86G was damaged but was rebuilt in time for the race. Anders Olofsson, Alain Ferte and Patrick Gonin had the car up to tenth place in the early running but Gonin crashed out in the night.

For 1988, March built two 88Gs for the Le Mans Company. One took part in the race, together with an 87G, both run by the Le Mans Company. One was driven by the ex-Interscope Hawaiian driver, Danny Ongais, with Michel Trolle and Toshio Suzuki, the other by Anders Olofsson, Lamberto Leoni and Akio Morimoto.

Sadly, both engines in the cars failed at 74 laps due to incorrect mapping of the fuel injection system. The V8 engine was redesigned by Nissan as was the 88G, this now having a longer wheelbase but it was a retrograde step. These cars were known as Nissan R88Es.

Another one of the R88Es and an up-dated 87G were sold to the Le Mans Company with V6 engines but the best results were 14th at Le Mans with an R88E being driven by Allan Grice, Win Percy and

NISSAN: THE GTP & GROUP C RACECARS 1984-1993

Mike Wilds. In Japan, the cars soldiered on in the All-Japan Sportscar Championship, but no great results were recorded.

For 1989, the FIA announced that teams wishing to enter Le Mans must compete in the World Championship. Nissan had negotiated with five different companies about production of their next Group C car, and eventually opted for Lola.

The design concept was Eric Broadley's. Lola's CAD/CAM system was heavily used (as evidenced by the excellent fitting of panels) in the design process by Andy Scriven, Clive Lark and Clive Cooper.

The Lola-Nissan prototype under test in England. [Photo: Courtesy of LAT.]

The R89C had a composite chassis of carbon fiber over Kevlar honeycomb with Nomex honeycomb being used in some areas that were difficult to shape. Aluminum honeycomb was used in the larger flat areas such as the floor. Front, rear and dash bulkheads were integral. This was actually the first carbon/composite chassis by Lola for a sportscar. A steel roll cage was fitted within the monocoque.

The car's shape was influenced by engine and brake cooling needs and

The Nissan V8 VRH35Z engine, seen here in one of the Lola-Nissan R89Cs. [Photo: Courtesy of Nissan.]

the Nissan styling department also put their design expertise into this area. The bodywork was made of simple fiberglass, as this lent itself to modification, which was anticipated during the car's development. The rear wheels were enclosed by removable covers, with winglets behind them. Horizontal skirts in sculpted recesses ran along the bottom sides of the car between the wheels. This was to improve airflow under the car. The rear wing was set at deck height for multi-functions, acting less as a wing, and more as a deflector for air from underneath the car.

The front radiator was almost horizontally positioned, fed by central ducts in the nose. Hot air was vented upwards through an aperture on top of the nose. Ducts at the bottom of the windshield fed cool air through tunnels flanking the cockpit to turbo intercoolers and oil coolers on both sides of the engine. With the exception of the length of the doors, the tunnels actually traveled inside the tub in the sponsons.

The fully stressed 3.5-liter DOHC V8 engine had twin IHI turbos. The cylinder banks were at a 90 degree angle and had 4 valve heads. Nissan's ECCS-R-NDIS management system was used, and power output was said to be approximately 800 bhp.

The 5-speed Hewland VGC transaxle with March ramp differential was mated to a specially-designed bellhousing/oil tank. The flanks of the gearbox case

Keith Greene, Team Manager for Nissan at Le Mans in 1986 and 1989. [Photo: Courtesy of Mercedes LAT.]

were machined smooth to form part of the diffuser wall. Suspension was by double wishbones all round, and coil spring/damper units were operated by push-rods. Front shock absorbers were mounted horizontally above the axle line; at the rear they were on top of the transmission. The clutch was a standard triple plate AP for Le Mans, but a carbon version was used for shorter races. The 14 inch Brembo brakes had four-piston calipers.

Laurie Bray again: "The R89C was a super car. It was very expensive to build. We (Lola) built six of them. Two went to Nissan Motorsport Europe and four went straight to Nissan in Japan. As a rolling chassis, without engine or electrical system, they cost in excess of a million pounds each. Not

The Lola-Nissan R89C on test at Snetterton in England. [Photo: Courtesy of LAT.]

only that, but Nissan ordered twenty-five spare noses, with lights and all the wiring too! By the way, that price didn't include any spare parts."

The Le Mans-spec. car was tested at Snetterton and Nissan's Arizona track, then Paul Ricard, where the sprint car also appeared. This had a more conventional two-tier rear wing, mounted higher, as well as larger volume diffuser tunnels.

The World Sports-Prototype Championship race program was now handled by Nissan Motorsport Europe, based in Milton Keynes. The very experienced Keith Greene was in charge under Howard Marsden and they hired young guns Mark Blundell and Julian Bailey as their initial driver pairing. Andrew Gilbert-Scott was hired as a sometime substitute. David Scotney was the Crew Chief.

As the new Lola-Nissan R89C was not ready in time for the early part of the season, Hasemi and Anders Oloffson drove this modified March 87G, fitted with a VRH30 V8 engine, in the World Championship opening round at Suzuka in April 1989. They finished in eleventh place. [Photo: Courtesy of Nissan.]

Lightning Speed

Masahiro Hasemi and Anders Olofsson R89C at Suzuka. [Photo: Courtesy of Nissan.]

Mark Blundell and Julian Bailey went to Ricard and Julian Bailey was the first to drive the new car. Mark Blundell: "That test didn't last long. After twenty minutes, Julian stuffed it into the Armco. Eric Broadley loved big sportscars, so this was really his baby. It was interesting to see his face when he learned about that! Of course, being an all-carbon tub, it had to go back to the factory to be repaired."

Julian Bailey also remembered that first test: "The R89C was a great car. Very together from the word go. First of all, I drove it without any bodywork, then they put that on and out I went. Of course, it had a lot of turbo lag and that can come and bite you. That's what it did at Ricard. I hit a lake on the straight and it snapped straight right and went in nose first. Eric Broadley was very interested to see the damage as it crash-tested the car straight away!"

"Eric's first words were: 'Very interesting test' when he looked over the car to inspect the damage. 'Course, Nissan was a works team, so they just rolled another car out of the transporter, they'd brought three or four with them. That's the difference between driving for a works and a private team."

"Howard Marsden was the boss of Nissan Motorsport Europe, and a nicer guy you couldn't wish to meet. He was the perfect gentleman. I wish there were more around like him. Yes, those were some of the happiest times of my life. You have to realize that we were just a bunch of young, very competitive kids back then."

Race debut of the Nissan was at Dijon's WSC round. By coincidence, it was also the debut of Nissan's rival Toyota, their program being run by Tom's Toyota of Great Britain. Johnny Dumfries put his Toyota 88C on the front row of the grid and finished fourth in the actual race. Bailey and Blundell qualified sixth, but their race was spoiled by two pitstops to replace the windshield, which kept popping out because of flexing on the bumpy track. This led to the screen fixing being later on improved. The car's main early problems were with the brakes, before a switch to carbon for July's Brands Hatch race.

Tires supplier Dunlop was getting left behind in gearing up for the radial technology used for the Group C cars. Dave Scotney, Crew Chief for the lead car, remembered: "That Lola Nissan was a cracking car. The R90C was a good evolution, but the basic design of the R89C was excellent. Trouble is, we were let down by the Dunlop tires, to whom Nissan were contracted. They were crap, there's no other word for it. If only we'd been on Goodyears!"

"The only way we could make the cars work on those tires was to let the drivers really boot it down the straights and almost tip-toe through the corners, because the tires were not up to the car's downforce and handling. Trouble was, that really screwed us on fuel consumption. There were no end of races where we had to back off towards the end to make the finish. Most of the times, we qualified on race tires, because the qualifiers were just too fragile and the drivers didn't trust them. I can remember one test at Monza where Julian Bailey had a rear tire let go at the exit of the Parabolica. That was a big moment for him! I pleaded with Howard Marsden, our boss, for

Left:
Mark Blundell
Below:
Julian Bailey.
[Photos: Courtesy of LAT.]

and Arie Luyendyk. It was discovered that the low Le Mans-spec wing had to be mounted higher to bring the center of pressure further back. As well, there was a March-Nissan R88S "Cougar" for Team Le Mans. This seems to have been the Ongais/Trolle/Suzuki car from 1988.

The cars qualified roughly ten seconds off the pole-winning pace of the Sauber-Mercedes, but qualifying pace has never been a priority at Le Mans, anyway.

Julian Bailey set off at a scorching pace, and was trying to wrest second place from John Nielsen's Jaguar at Mulsanne on the fifth lap. The cars came together when Bailey hit the Jaguar from behind, and the

different tires, but all he could say was: 'Sorry, we're contracted to Dunlop and that's that.'"

Le Mans witnessed a concerted onslaught with three cars entered by Nissan. Bailey and Blundell were joined by Martin Donnelly in one R89C, whilst the Japanese trio of Masahiro Hasemi, Katsuyoshi Hoshino and Toshio Suzuki drove the second car. The third car was entrusted to the Electramotive crew of Geoff Brabham, Chip Robinson

Le Mans, France June 10th, 1989: Immaculate preparation. The Nissan Motorsport Europe entries at Le Mans in 1989. [Photo: Courtesy of LAT.]

resultant damage put the lead Nissan out of the race.

Julian Bailey: "For me, the race was twenty-four minutes, not twenty-four hours. I wasn't flavor of the month with Nissan after hitting John Nielsen, in fact Howard Marsden told me that it was only the fact that I'd taken the Mulsanne Kink flat out at

Le Mans 1989. The Nissans were every bit as fast as the Mercedes, Jaguar and Porsche opposition but a series of misfortunes kept them out of the top three. [Photo: Courtesy of LAT.]

Headlights piercing the darkness, one of the NME entered Lola-Nissan R89C's seen during the night at Le Mans. [Photo: Courtesy of LAT.]

248 mph, that saved my job. I can remember doing it and thinking – if this goes off here, it's going to be a big accident! I don't think I could do it now."

The Cougar car climbed to fourth after a steady start, but retired in the small hours of the night, when its engine expired. John Knepp had provided the V6 engines for the team: "At Le Mans, we were all using four-star gas. We qualified sixth. The Japanese management set us a bogey time that was far slower than the car could run. They didn't want their V8's shown up. At the first pit stop, we were 13th, but our fuel allocation would have allowed us to run twenty-seven hours at that pace. We knew

With the coming of the V8 engined Lola-Nissans, great things were expected of the team at Le Mans. Sadly, none finished the race. This R89C was driven by the Japanese team of Masahiro Hasemi, Kazuyoshi Hoshino and Toshio Suzuka. The engine failed after ten hours. [Photo: Courtesy of LAT.]

that we were in with a chance of winning."

"I'll never forget seeing Jurgen Barth wandering down pitlane, checking everyone's fuel consumption. When he came to us, he walked on, but then the realization of the figures struck him and he spun around and gaped at our Nissan!"

Electramotive's trio then took up

the challenge. They held fifth place in the morning, but sudden loss of oil pressure was a sign of serious engine damage, and their run came to an end, too.

Geoff Brabham remembered Le Mans well: "It's difficult to compare the Lola-built 1989 and 1990 V-8 Nissans with the Electramotive/NPTI V-6 cars. The first year that we did Le Mans (1989) we just turned up as drivers for another team. That was the last year of the Mulsanne straight without the chicanes. The Lola-Nissan

Masahiro Hasemi and Andres Olofsson shared this R89C at Suzuka. [Photo: Courtesy of Nissan.]

Podium finish. Mark Blundell and Julian Bailey drove the R89C to third place at Donington, showing how far the team had progressed in just one year of International Sports Car racing. [Photo: Courtesy of LAT.]

R89C's we drove had very little downforce to allow them to run fast on the straight, so they were nothing like the high-downforce Electramotive cars that I was driving in America. In fact, they were not very nice."

Jarama next, and this was tackled by Bailey and Blundell in a brand new chassis, but brought little reward as they struggled through to a delayed eighth, five laps behind the winning Sauber-Mercedes C9.

For the Brands Hatch WS-PC round the car was equipped with carbon brakes. To allow better cooling for them the rear wheel covers had been removed. The car had a peculiar combination of Dunlop tires with 17 inch diameter crossplies at the front and 19 inch diameter radials at the rear! This worked, though, and the drivers liked the handling.

The changes seemed to untap the car's potential; Bailey qualified it fourth and charged to second in the race, before spinning into a gravel trap after just 19 laps.

That same weekend Masahiro Hasemi put one of the Le Mans cars on pole at Fuji for an All-Japan Sports Prototype Championship race. Tire failure curtailed his race, however.

Mark Blundell again: "That car was mighty fast. We were only let down by two things; the tires, which weren't the tires to have, and the fuel consumption. Time after time we would lead the Mercedes, but we would have to back off to try and make the finish. I reckon that if we had had the right tires, we could have improved our lap times by over a second a lap."

"Don't forget that this Lola-Nissan was the first Group C car to have carbon brakes in 1989. By 1990, most of the top teams were using carbon."

"The Lola-Nissan had considerable downforce and balance-wise, it was pretty good, except for understeer. You can see that as the car was developed, the front splitter changed and we got vents over the front wheels to try and get the air out as it built up in the front wheel arches and contributed to the understeering problem that we had. I always reckon that, without a major re-design, no matter what the engineers do, the car will always feature its initial handling. That understeer was an inbuilt factor of the car's handling."

"Overall, though, you had to say that the Lola-Nissan was a pretty good car. It was certainly great fun and a mighty quick car to drive. The ride wasn't wonderful but I guess that the tires had a lot to do with that."

Martin Donnelly was the one to score the R89C's first victory. He was entered in the German SAT1 SuperCup event on the Diepholz airfield circuit. He qualified second to Bob Wollek's Porsche, but managed to beat the mainly Porsche opposition in the sprint race.

Back in the WS-PC Bailey was paired with Andrew Gilbert-Scott for the Nürburgring event. They qualified fourth (again!), and Gilbert-Scott managed to pass the Saubers in his opening stint. Bailey then stretched their advantage to thirty seconds at the end of his stint but in his second stint, he had to back off to make the fuel allocation last the distance. This dropped the Nissan to third place close to the finish. Bailey was ordered to stop before the finish line to wait for the last lap, which he did, but even then the tank ran dry on that final tour and he wasn't classified as a finisher, due to the 400% rule covering the last lap.

Julian Bailey: "Well, we were never told if the fuel would last out in the race itself. I guess we worried the Germans though! Of course, the Sauber-Mercedes had the advantage of those 5-liter engines versus our 3.5-liter units and they had lots more torque as well having better fuel consumption."

Jean-Louis Schlesser, Mercedes' lead driver, later told David Scotney that the Mercedes top brass were not best pleased at being led for much of the race at their "home" track by an English car with a Japanese engine!

Blundell was back for Donington, where the car started from third place on the grid and was involved in a four-car battle for the lead during the early stages. Bailey pushed to the fore on lap thirty-seven and the Nissan led the field for over fifty laps. During the second pitstop the crew were forced to suffer a seventeen-second penalty for fuel going in too quickly during their first stop. A slow puncture delayed them further, but they only lost second place three laps before the finish, Bailey hanging on to take third with an almost completely worn-through tire. They finished on the same lap as the victorious Mercedes-badged Saubers, though.

At Spa the car was a handful as the crossply/radial tire combination did not work in the wet practice. Still, from seventh on the grid Bailey and Blundell were to inherit third in the dry race, when second placed Jean-Louis Schlesser's Sauber-Mercedes ran out of fuel on the last lap. Bailey took fourth on the opening lap, but fell back as the crew had installed an "economy" chip into the engine management system.

The car again proved a handful on Mexico City's notoriously bumpy Hermanos Rodriguez circuit. Qualifying in eighth, the Nissan R89C had a troubled outing, where it never got higher than fourth place. Delayed by fuel pressure problems and out of the points, they were left with fifth place in the Team's World Championship. Bailey and Blundell were joint eleventh in the Drivers' Series.

There was to be no joy in Japan, either, although Anders Olofsson led early on in a late season race at Suzuka, but crashed. Julian Bailey had also taken in a SAT1 SuperCup event at the Nürburgring, where a bad misfire restricted him to third place.

[Photo: Courtesy of LAT.]

R89C (Lola design)

89C-01:

1989:
21/5: Dijon: Bailey/Blundell/Donnelly, #23; 15th.
10/6-11/6: Le Mans 24-Hours: Bailey/Blundell/ Donnelly, #24; DNF. (Susp.)
Dave Scotney – Crew Chief.
23/7: Brands Hatch: Bailey/Gilbert-Scott, #23; DNF. (Accident.)
17/9: Spa-Francorchamps: Bailey/Blundell/ Gilbert-Scott, #23; 3rd.

1990:
08/4: Suzuka: Hasemi/Olofsson, #24; 3rd.
16/6-17/6: Courage entry at Le Mans. Regout/ Cudini/Los, #82; 22nd.

89C-02:

1989: 4250 cc V8 Turbo.
10/6-11/06: Le Mans 24-Hours: Brabham/ Robinson/Luyendyk, #25; DNF.
23/7: 500 Miles of Fuji: Hoshino/Suzuki, #23; DNF. (Electrics.)
8/10: 1000 km Fuji: Hoshino/Suzuki, #23; DNF. (Accident.)
03/12: Suzuka 1000 km: Hoshino/Suzuki; DNF. (Accident.)

1990:
08/4: Suzuka: Hoshino/Gilbert-Scott/Suzuki, #23; NRF.

89C-03: Team Le Mans.

1989:
09/4: Suzuka: Hasemi/Olofsson, #24; 11th.
30/4: 1000 km Fuji: Olofsson/Hasemi, #24; 3rd.
10/6-11/6: Le Mans 24-Hours: Hasemi/ Hoshino/Suzuki, #23; DNF.
23/7: 500 Miles of Fuji: Hasemi/Olofsson, #85; DNF. (Tire.)
8/10: 1000 km Fuji: Hasemi/Olofsson, #24; 8th.
3/12: 1000 km Suzuka: Hasemi/Olofsson, #24; 10th.

1990:
16/6-17/6: Le Mans 24-Hours: Wada/Olofsson/ Sala, #85; DNF. (Electrics.)

89C-04:

1989:
25/6: Jarama: Bailey/Blundell, #23; 8th.
22/7: Dijon: Acheson/Brancatelli, #24; DNF.
20/8: Nürburgring: Gilbert-Scott/Bailey, #23; NRF. (Out of fuel, but 8th.)
03/9: Donington: Bailey/Blundell, #23; 3rd.
29/10: Mexico City: Bailey/Blundell, #23; 12th.

89C-05:   Nothing known.

89C-06:   Nothing known.

Nissan R89C Nismo (WSPC 1989)

Chassis	Monocoque in carbon fiber and synthetic materials. Designed by Paul Bailey, built by Lola Cars, England. 6 built.
Bodywork	Kevlar and Carbon Fiber.
Engine	Nissan VRH35Z 90 degree V8. Four valves per cylinder. 2 x IHI turbochargers.
Bore x Stroke	85 x 77 mm = 3496 cc.
Compression	8.5:1.
Power	800 bhp @ 7600 rpm.
Torque	80 mkg @ 5600 rpm.
Electronic Engine Management	ECCS-R-NDIS.
Gearbox	Hewland VGC with 5 forward, 1 reverse gears.
Weight	910 kg.
Wheelbase	2794 mm.
Length	4800 mm.
Width	1990 mm.
Height	1100 mm.
Tires	Dunlop.
Max. Speed	380 kph plus.

1990 World Championship

4

Kazuyoshi Hoshino and Andrew Gilbert-Scott drove this Lola-Nissan R89/90C in the WSPC round at Suzuka in 1990. They qualified in fifth place but failed to finish. [Photo: Courtesy of Nissan.]

A refinement of the R89C, the R90C version had a stiffer chassis structure with reduced internal dimensions and right angle joins replacing curved ones in the monocoque. Laurie Bray: "The R90C was very similar to the R89C, but a significant point is that we made it easier to get at the steering rack. The R89C had been difficult in this area." The aerodynamics were slightly modified. Outwardly, the R90C could be identified by a new nose shape.

There was also a subtly different engine cover, but this was almost unnoticeable. Detail modifications had been carried out to the suspension for greater wheel movement. It was felt that, in the interests of maximizing efficiency of the underbody aerodynamics, the designers of the R89C had gone slightly over the top in this.

The gearbox had a new one-piece casing, which allowed for wider tunnels underneath the car, and there was now a semi-dry sump modification to the box, too. AP Racing carbon brakes replaced the Brembo ones. The engine specification was now VRH35Z and the NME cars were to run Dunlop's latest radial tires. The European version of this new car was dubbed R90C.

At Nissan Motorsport Europe, Keith Greene left, to be replaced by Dave Price and Bob Bell from Sauber. Dave Price, realizing that the Lola chassis was not quick enough to do the job, enlisted Bell to set up a design office to design an all-new car for 1991.

Bob Bell: "I left Sauber-Mercedes at the end of 1989 because Jochen Neerpasch wanted me to move over to the design side of the Sauber-Mercedes race program. I just wanted to go racing, so when Dave [Price] told me that Nissan were offering phenomenal money to run their team, I went too."

"The R90C was not a bad car. When it first arrived, we found that the gearbox

New broom: Dave Price, assisted by Bob Bell, replaced the outgoing Keith Greene as Team Manager of the NME team in 1990. [Photo: Courtesy of LAT.]

lacked reverse gear. Now the rules for sports car racing clearly state that reverse is needed, and so Lola had to set to and provide a reverse gear in the box. I had to stop Eric Broadley from designing a whole new gearbox!"

"Nissan's V8 engine was a developed copy of the Cosworth DFV. When I flew to Nissan's factory in Japan, I noticed that some of the Nissan V8's engine used English measurements. When I looked around, I found two Cosworths in their engine shop. One had been cut up to take a closer look at the parts, the other was the one the engineers had run on the dyno. They didn't make any secret of it. How else could they have short-circuited developing a racing V8?"

Kenny Acheson and Gianfranco Brancatelli joined the driver squad in order to be able to run two cars at each WS-PC meeting.

David Scotney again: "The Lola-Nissan R90C was a good car but we were still bedeviled by Dunlop tires. On the mechanical front, everything was fine, those engines were exceedingly reliable. We would do two test days and two race meetings on the same engine, whilst TWR and Toyota were having to change their V6's after every session!"

Mike Gue, who headed Essex Racing at the time and today has close ties with Nissan (he is helping today's historic racers with their Nissans), was told by Nissan's engineers that: "You can run the engines flat-out for sixty hours. They will not break."

The R90CP debuted at Fuji's All-Japan Sports Prototype Championship round, where Masahiro Hasemi qualified it second, while its sister works car was slotted fourth by Hoshino and the Le Mans

Hoshino drives the R90C at Suzuka in 1990. [Photo: Courtesy of Nissan.]

Company's private R89C was gridded in sixth place. The works cars held their positions in the race, which was won by the new works Toyota.

The WS-PC also opened in Japan, where Nissan was represented in the Suzuka race by the same cars that took the start at Fuji. Andrew Gilbert-Scott replaced Toshio

Suzuki, who was unwell, as Hoshino's partner. Hoshino qualified fifth, in his 89-chassis'd but R90CP bodied car, which was using carbon brakes for the first time in Japan. In the race the crew was forced into economy mode and eventually the car ended up stuck in the gravel after an off.

Masahiro Hasemi qualified the second works car ninth, still sporting 89-style bodywork. On the race's first lap he was slightly delayed by a skirmish resulting from the tardy start of Jochen Mass in a Sauber-Mercedes, but he steadily worked up the order. Co-driver Anders Olofsson

Hoshino and Gilbert-Scott drove this R90CP at Suzuka for the 300 mile race in April. Although qualifying well in fifth place, they retired in the race. [Photo: Courtesy of Nissan.]

Monza was the NME team's first appearance in the WS-PC. [Photo: Courtesy of LAT.]

climbed to fifth place, which eventually became third, as one of the Toyotas was called in for a stop-and-go penalty, and then Martin Brundle's TWR Jaguar expired with engine failure at only five laps from the finish.

At the flag, Hasemi and Olofsson were one lap behind the two works Sauber-Mercedes. The private R89C was not really on the pace, and its race ended when Kenny Acheson was unceremoniously punted off.

John Knepp: "The V8 engine, in my opinion, was too heavy and had too much inertia. It also broke crankshafts and we [Electramotive] made new ones out of various exotic materials."

"Poor Hasemi's engine always seemed to break, and he was a very diligent guy, very mechanically sympathetic. In the end, the Japanese management demanded Don Devendorf's presence at a race in Japan and he noticed that each team did their own wiring. He rightly guessed that it was electronic interference with the management system that was causing the failures and further research proved him right."

The R90CK debuted in the first European WS-PC race of the season at Monza.

The cars qualified sixth and seventh at Monza. In the race, Blundell and Brancatelli benefited from a first lap shunt to run third for a while, but in the last stints the Nissans were down to fifth and sixth. Acheson and Bailey were delayed by a stop to attend to a loose front wheel, dropping to seventh at the end. Blundell and Brancatelli did not make it to the finish, running out of fuel, as the team had been caught out with telemetry troubles.

At Silverstone Blundell qualified fourth and Bailey seventh. This time the Nissans worked up the order to scrap for second place in the last driving stints, albeit a full lap behind the leading TWR Jaguar. Just ten laps from the finish Bailey's car suffered a broken rocker in the rear suspension, which put it out of the race. Blundell was once more forced to conserve fuel towards the finish, letting the second Jaguar past into second place. He still ran dry. Julian managed to cross the finish line on the starter motor, but was not classified, as his last lap had taken too long to complete. A recurrence of the telemetry problems had let the team down.

The drivers were not entirely happy with their understeering cars at Spa, where Blundell qualified fifth and Bailey tenth. On a wet but drying track the team's tire strategy of starting on cut intermediates and pitting early for slicks proved a good choice though, moving the Nissans into second and third by the time of the first driver changes.

In the middle stint Brancatelli's car started losing power and Blundell eventually brought their car to the finish a struggling tenth. Bailey and Acheson, too, lost some ground, but inherited third place when one of the Jaguars dropped out and they held the position to the finish, staying on the same lap as Jochen Mass and Karl Wendlinger in the winning Sauber-Mercedes.

Le Mans saw a massive attack from Nissan with no less than seven entries. NME had their two usual cars with Martin Donnelly and Olivier Grouillard complimenting the driving squad.

NPTI had two similar R90CKs for Geoff Brabham/Chip Robinson/Derek Daly and Bob Earl/Michael Roe/Steve Millen. NPTI had carried out an extensive test program with the help of personnel from the abandoned Aston Martin Group C project, led by Ray Mallock.

The cars had detail modifications, such as suspension adapted to the Goodyear tires, which the team ran in place of NME's

Le Mans, 1990: Nissan fielded a seven car team in a massive onslaught on Sports Car racing's most prestigious race. [Photo: Courtesy of LAT.]

Dunlops. NISMO brought their own R90CP, the distinctively bodied Japanese series regular, for Masahiro Hasemi/Katsuyoshi Hoshino/Toshio Suzuki. Team Le Mans also had the car they ran in Japan, an R89C for Takao Wada/Anders Olofsson/Maurizio Sandro Sala. The local Courage team fielded an R89C for Herve Regout, Alain Cudini, Costas Los in addition to two cars of their own manufacture. Their Nissan's rear suspension was modified, as the team used 17 inch Goodyear tires instead of 18 inch.

The Le Mans circuit had been altered with two chicanes on the Mulsanne straight, which placed new demands on the cars. The R90CKs' aerodynamics were closer to sprint spec, because top speed was no longer such a priority. NME and Nismo had taken the decision to run carbon-carbon brakes, while NPTI used iron discs with carbon-metallic pads.

Don Devendorf of Electramotive: "NISMO in Japan sent us two R90C's. The first thing that we found under testing was

In the pits: The Nissan R89Ck of Geoff Brabham, Chip Robinson and Derek Daly. Leading halfway through, they were put out with a split fuel tank. [Photo: Courtesy of LAT.]

Early on at Le Mans, the "Japanese" crewed car of Masahiro Hasemi, Kazuyoshi Hoshino and Toshio Suzuki leads the Julian Bailey, Mark Blundell and Gianfranco Brancatelli-driven car. [Photo: Courtesy of LAT.]

that the carbon fiber floor was too thin at the front. This, coupled with a mechanical linkage problem, meant that the pressure exerted on the brake pedal from the driver's foot changed as the floor flexed. The European teams hadn't figured that out. We cut out the floor and strengthened it with steel, plus we also cured the brake linkage problem. I remember Eric Broadley being intrigued by the hump over the front panel!"

Trevor Harris: "There was a year, 1989, when the English team, NME, ran a car at Le Mans. Wes Moss, Don and I went to Le Mans that year to observe. Then, in 1990, we [Electramotive] went and ran a car while Dave Price ran the NME team. It was all very political."

LIGHTNING SPEED

"Yes, I remember the Lola-Nissan R90C. That car was pretty good, very fast, with a good downforce to drag ratio. We were supposed to be running Le Mans in 1990, but had never tested the car before we accepted to do the program. We started developing the car in the US, and we hired Ray Mallock and his shop in the UK to help and that became our English outpost."

"The car went to Ray. He's a very able guy. Don and I went to the first test session at Donington. I think Julian Bailey was driving. There was a serious braking problem with the R90C. It didn't stop.

Masahiro Hasemi, Kazuyoshi Hoshino and Toshio Suzuki gave Nissan their best finish in 1990, fifth overall. [Photo: Courtesy of LAT.]

The engine was terrific but ... anyway, the mechanical ratios of the pedal assembly were wrong. Also, the floor around the pedal box was too flexible. We ended up doing a brake pressure test and found that there was really very little, about 600 pound. We wanted 1000 at the calipers and so I redesigned it and the work was done at Ray Mallock's shop."

"We ran a test at Silverstone in a downpour. It was worthless, so we couldn't do any effective testing. There was no more time to test the brakes before Le Mans itself."

By Sunday morning, the Japanese-crewed R90C was one of the few Nissans still running. [Photo: Courtesy of LAT.]

Inside the Le Man pole-setting Nissan's cockpit. Still very much as it was in 1990, R90C-03 is today raced in HSR events and is still ferociously fast. [Photo: Author's collection.]

"So we went to Le Mans with an unknown package. We had a plan for changing the pads. We were using US Perfect Friction Brake pads. They had developed a very good carbon pad for iron brakes. At Le Mans we had quite a driver roster over there with Geoff Brabham and Julian Bailey amongst the hot shoes."

"After the first evening of running, we were the fastest. Steve Millen had driven a GTO car for us and is a very, very good driver. That engine was capable of a lot of horsepower. Trouble was, we weren't supposed to be the fastest! It was made very clear to us that the wrong car had done the quickest time at first. The wrong team had done well! Really distressing! There were a lot of glum Japanese faces that night."

"Unfortunately, Le Mans 1990 turned out to be US v UK. Nissan's management didn't do things well, and they promoted the rivalry. The Management were not racing people. They were from other departments and had been put into the racing area. It was a strange strategy. We should have worked together. Dave Price and Bob Bell are good guys."

"It all finished up in an adversarial situation and they had information that we all could have shared. That wasn't the way it was done. Still, we had a lot of fun, leading the race at the half-way mark and being well up on our fuel consumption. Then we were put out by a fuel bag leak. The European guys had had the same problem, but they didn't tell us and we didn't know about it."

Kas Kastner: "I remember us going to Le Mans in 1990 as part of Nissan's seven car team. Of course, there we were running one of the Lola-built R90Cs. Geoff Brabham set the fastest time on race tires in the first night practice." *(This was before Mark Blundell's run – Author.)* "I remember testing at Riverside particularly. Through the kink there, the car sounded like a B-17 on a low-level pass. Geoff Brabham was timed at 208 mph there."

Mark Blundell caused a stir in qualifying, by putting a Nissan on the pole by the overwhelming margin of six seconds. For this purpose his engine was boosted to give over 1000 bhp.

The Nismo car's aerodynamics obviously worked, as it recorded the highest straightline speed of all at 366 kph. Dave Price: "Tetsu Ikusawa, the engineering man, had had a special qualifying engine built. Trouble was, in the qualifying run itself, the wastegate jammed shut and that gave the engine a lot more power than intended! I'm sure we were getting well over a thousand horses."

"I remember the Japanese technicians frantically telling me to stop the run but Mark was going so well, I thought why bother? Let him finish the lap. I have a photograph of Mark with his foot hard in it under acceleration and you can see that his helmet's right back on the headrest, with it being forced up his chin, such is the acceleration."

Montreal, Canada. Another strong second place finish for the Nissan of Mark Blundell and Julian Bailey, but Nissan had already decided to withdraw from WS-PC racing by this time. [Photo: Courtesy of LAT.]

Mark Blundell, the driver of the epic lap later told the author: "The problem was that the car was strictly a qualifying car with the engine a hand grenade. All week we ran it and that engine never ran cleanly and the mechanics were working on it constantly. Finally, it was qualifying time. We waited for dusk, which gave the best possible conditions for a turbo car and I went out. I had no real clue as to the power that the engine was boosted to, it was a real shot in the dark, so to say."

"I had to poodle around an entire lap to keep the tires cool until I booted it coming out of the second chicane. I went sideways up the road and it spun the wheels all the way up to fourth gear. Through the chicanes, I was lock to lock with it. I have an in-cockpit video of that lap somewhere and it's pretty exciting. I heard afterwards that the Japanese engineers had been shouting at Dave (Price) to tell me to slow down and bring it back for another go but somehow, my radio disconnected itself and I couldn't hear anyone on it. Strangely, it worked when I got back to the pits!"

"I was told afterwards that we hit 237 mph between the chicanes and it certainly felt bloody quick. I think, if I had had another shot at it, I could have knocked another one to two seconds off that time. Don't forget that that was the only lap we did in that car with all the power being usable. The engineers reckoned it was putting out eleven hundred horsepower."

David Scotney: "Yeah, that was some lap. When we heard the time, we thought the timing people had got it wrong, or Mark had jumped one of the chicanes! Funnily enough, Mark didn't seem to think he'd gone much quicker than before until we showed him the time sheet. He just reckoned the car had more grunt than before. I was a very proud man when the grid formed up and there we were on pole position at Le Mans in a British car."

"In the race itself, we were going well until the car broke its gear cluster, luckily in the pits, so we were able to fix that. Later, that car went out with the gearshift rod broken. Brancatelli had an off that cost us a couple of laps whilst we replaced the nose, too."

Kenny Acheson. [Photo: Courtesy of LAT.]

Hasemi placed his car third on the grid and with Brabham and Acheson securing the next slots the front of the field had a distinctly Nissan look about it at the start.

Bob Bell remembered Le Mans, 1990, well. "Mark Blundell's pole lap. The Japanese engineers were very protective of their super-boosted engine. If anything had gone wrong with it, we had to say that it had been a chassis failure. Certainly, I can remember the Japanese technicians telling Dave to stop him (Mark Blundell) but we just told them that he was on a qualifying lap and couldn't hear us above the engine noise!"

"The NPTI R90C came fitted with steel brakes, instead of the carbon ones that we'd been using. They were having a

The normal "long-distance" rear wing as fitted to R90C-03. Compare how much less area this has compared to the "spring" format rear wing of R90C-07. It was this reduced downforce that allowed Mark Blundell to set such a staggering speed on his pole position qualifying lap at Le Mans in 1990. [Photo: Author's collection.]

The double-tier wing of R90C-07. After 1990, the car was reconfigured as an R91C by having the doors blended into the body, so that the driver must enter through the opening side window. Also, the rear wing was reconfigured thus to give extra downforce to help it in shorter "sprint" type races of the Japanese Sportscar Championship. the resultant increase in drag was though worth the trade-off in top speed.
[Photo: Author's collection.]

dreadful time with the pedal-box flexing. Carbone Industries didn't want us to run the carbon brakes, in case they failed during the 24-Hours and someone got hurt. I told their representative: 'If you don't supply us, we'll withdraw from the race and I'll issue a press release blaming your company for the withdrawal!' Bit heavy, but what else could I do? Luckily, they gave in."

Nissan's attack suffered its first setback before the race was even underway. Kenny Acheson was sidelined on the formation lap with crown wheel and pinion failure.

For 1991, the very last R90C built was sold to the Nova FromA-sponsored racing team and hosted some impressive results in the Japanese Sportscar Championship, driven by Volker Weidler and and A. Nakaya. In 1992 it finished eighth in the Daytona 24-Hours, and then went back to Japan to be raced until the end of the season by, amongst others, Heinz Harald Frentzen and Mauri Martini. [Photo: Courtesy of Daniel Mainzer.]

Julian Bailey, in the pole-winning car, led from the start but gave way to Oscar Larrauri's Porsche on lap four. These two were setting the pace, while Hasemi held off four TWR Jaguars in third. Mark Blundell, having taken over from Bailey, retook the lead in the second hour and the car stayed at the front until Gianfranco Brancatelli had a high-speed collision with the Toyota of Larrousse-Lola F1 driver Aguri Suzuki in the fifth hour. The Italian lost a lot of time crawling back to the pits with a puncture and damaged nose. Despite working their way back to the lead lap, the crew's work was in vain: They retired with transmission failure in the small hours of the night. Brancatelli's delay left an NPTI car with Geoff Brabham at the wheel in the lead. A brake pad change in the sixth hour lost this crew almost a lap, but they were back out front shortly after, when Alain Ferte's leading Jaguar retired.

Geoff Brabham, Chip Robinson and Derek Daly all had their share at the wheel, leading into the night, until another pad change dropped them to second, behind the TWR Jaguar of John Nielsen, Price Cobb and Martin Brundle. These two cars ran very close to each other for a couple of hours until a telemetry glitch brought caution into the Nissan's progress and they backed off slightly.

The NPTI car was still in a strong second place in the morning, when a fuel leak in the bag tank first delayed them in the pits and then ended their run for good.

Geoff Brabham: "In 1990, at Le Mans, we drove an R90C Lola-Nissan that NPTI had prepared. I remember that the engine was very good. We were leading in the middle of the night and were bang on our fuel mileage but the Jaguars had exceeded theirs and we knew that they would have to drop back. Then the fuel bag split and put us out. That was very disappointing."

The NISMO entry had settled to a steady pace after the hectic early laps. It was delayed by a broken spring/damper mounting and crawled to the finish with serious gearbox troubles, having lost second, third and fourth gears. Hasemi, Hoshino and Suzuki were still classified fifth in the lone R90CP and might have been as high as second without their problems. The Nielsen/Cobb/Brundle Jaguar held on to the lead through the night and was out of reach of the Japanese crew by daybreak.

None of the other Nissans really figured. Earl, Roe and Millen in the second NPTI entry were delayed by a water leak and eventually sidelined with gearbox problems, although Bob Earl had the distinction of setting the fastest lap. Wada, Olofsson and Sala also suffered gearbox problems, but their race ended with engine failure. The Courage run Regout, Cudini and Los car suffered a catalogue of problems – including a gearbox rebuild, which took over an hour – but made the finish in a lowly twenty-second.

Bob Bell: "Yeah, well, after that defeat at Le Mans, it was all over. Nissan management just wanted to finish the race program right there. Pricey (Dave Price) had to almost plead with them to let us finish the European season. It was a shame, really. Nissan were in year two of their program.

The rear suspension attached to the gearbox of the R90C. Note the crossed-over coil spring/damper units.
[Photo: Author's collection.]

Everyone in racing knows that it takes three years to get to win races. Nissan thought that they could just throw money at the project, but you don't win Le Mans just by throwing money at it."

For the next WS-PC round, NME reshuffled their driver pairings, Bailey and Blundell getting together again and new boys Acheson and Brancatelli sharing the other car. They qualified sixth and ninth, respectively. Acheson's race was spoiled by a spin on oil, which resulted in sufficient damage to put the handling off for the rest of the race.

Bailey, on the other hand, had a strong start, climbing to third with genuine passing maneuvers in the first five laps. There was not much he or Blundell could do about the two fleeing Sauber-Mercedes at the front, but they held their third place with ease, scoring a good podium finish for Nissan.

That same weekend, Hasemi and Olofsson took a victory from pole at Fuji, in the second round of the Japanese series. This result was slightly fortuitous, as Hitoshi Ogawa's Toyota broke its engine, when it seemed poised for victory. Hoshino and Suzuki in the other NISMO car were third and Wada and Nakako in the private R89C were sixth.

At the Nürburgring's WS-PC race both NME Nissans had been fitted with small spoilers in the front corners to cure understeer. The cars qualified eighth and ninth, but the team unfortunately omitted to send Julian Bailey out in official qualifying, which meant he couldn't take part in the race.

Mark Blundell drove for the full 2 hours 40 minutes duration of the race, making it to fifth at the end, but three laps behind the victorious Sauber-Mercedes cars. Acheson and Brancatelli were slowed by their tires losing pressure and a consequent puncture to finish ninth.

In Japan, Kazuyoshi Hoshino and Toshio Suzuki won for Nissan in the local series' most prestigious round, the Suzuka 1000 kms. Their car had been switched to Bridgestone tires and the Dunlop shod sister car of Hasemi/Olofsson could not keep in touch.

Back in WS-PC, it was Kenny Acheson's turn to be the fastest qualifier of the NME drivers at Donington. He took fifth place on the grid, bumping Bailey and Blundell into sixth. Bailey stormed to second at the start, but was unable to hang on. The pair fought with the Spice of Tim Harvey and Cor Euser for fourth, but dropped back with fading brakes and had to give way to Acheson and Brancatelli, too. The Nissans finished fifth and seventh on the road, but both benefited by one position, when the Jaguars were excluded for a refueling infringement. The two Sauber-Mercedes were first and second, once again.

Kenny Acheson told the author: "After a year driving for Sauber-Mercedes, the Nissan was the second-best car out there. I actually think that it was better than the TWR-Jaguars. If only Nissan had got its act together. There were all sorts of political problems amongst the various factions in the Nissan Empire. I just had to take a step back and say to myself: 'This isn't what it was like last year'."

"The engine was great, the car could have done with some development but the tires! If Michelin were a year or two behind Goodyear, then Dunlop were fifteen years behind them. Still, Nissan should have been able to match the Sauber-Mercedes with the new car that Dave Price was developing."

In Montreal the Nissans were in good shape after an exclusive test. Blundell qualified second, benefiting from the use of qualifying tires, for once, while Acheson had to be content with ninth. In a race punctuated by two pace-car periods, Blundell dropped back a little, but during the second pace-car session pitted for less fuel than the main opposition and was, therefore, well placed at the restart. With Bailey at the wheel, they actually took the lead soon after the pace-car pulled off. They were now forced to save fuel, however, and Bailey was powerless to fend off the charging Mauro Baldi's Sauber-Mercedes. Just two laps after Baldi had taken the lead the race was stopped, when a manhole cover became detached and caused an accident involving three cars. Acheson had stayed in his car for the duration and was lying fifth, when the red flag came out. Half points were awarded, because of the early stoppage.

On the other side of the Globe, Masahiro Hasemi and Anders Olofsson clinched the All-Japan title for Nissan by winning at Sugo. Hoshino and Suzuki were fourth this time.

The drivers' title remained to be decided at the last Fuji race. Hasemi and Hoshino claimed the front row of the grid. The two R90CPs set off to do battle on slicks with drops of rain falling. Even the private R89C got in on the act, holding second for a while, but its transmission played up before half distance. Anders Olofsson took the wheel from Hasemi, but spun on his first lap out of the pits and got stuck in a gravel bed, losing some ten laps. Still, Hoshino and Suzuki couldn't hold on to the lead and the Toyota of Roland Ratzenberger and Naoki Nagasaka was ahead when the race was stopped after an accident to Johnny Herbert's Porsche. Hoshino and Suzuki were second, about a minute behind, and Hasemi and Olofsson were classified fifth. This, amazingly, led to all four works Nissan drivers being equal on points, but Hasemi and Olofsson were champions as they'd had two wins to the other crew's one!

The last WS-PC round of 1990 took place on the same weekend in Mexico City. Bailey and Acheson claimed fifth and seventh on the grid. Bailey followed the two Sauber-Mercs and the faster Jaguar early on,

The close confines of R90C-07's cockpit, showing the simple Stack dash layout and supported shoulder straps. In a long-distance race, the less a driver needs to pay attention to in the cockpit, the better! [Photo: Author's collection.]

but pitted early to take a relatively light load of fuel, so emerged in the lead, when the others had pitted, too. The Mercs came steaming past and Blundell and Bailey then had to ease off to save fuel, but they held on to third anyway, and eventually got second, when the fastest Mercedes was disqualified for having taken on too much fuel, just like the Jaguars at Donington. Brancatelli and Acheson suffered minor delays on their way to fifth, which similarly became fourth. Nissan finished third in the Makes Championship, not too distant from second placed Jaguar. Bailey, Blundell and Acheson were ninth, tenth and eleventh in the Drivers' standings.

It had been a season not without promise, but Nissan decided not to continue in the World Series in 1991. The boss of Nissan UK did not approve of money being spent on racing cars and the NME operation was closed down. Dave Price again: "I had been head-hunted from Sauber-Mercedes with a three-year contract to run the Nissan Motorsports operation. Instead, after just one year, I found myself having to tell everyone that they were out of work before Christmas."

Julian Bailey: "I would say that we were second-best after the Mercs. That was a great period in Sports-Car racing, 1989-90, with the Mercs, Nissans, Jags and the rest. You could still win if you were lucky in a privateer Porsche 962. We were very well paid and looked after. I remember going testing at Philip Island with Mark (Blundell), we came back first class because we could afford it. I loved driving with Mark, and with the Lola-Nissan team. They had a five-year plan but it fell apart with the coming of the 3.5 atmo formula."

NPTI and NISMO carried on in their respective fields, however, and the 1991 Daytona 24 Hours saw the Californian team enter three ex-Le Mans R90CKs. The race allowed Group C entries, although it was estimated these would have to run 2 seconds/lap quicker than IMSA opposition to compensate for their longer pitstops. There was also a regulation reserving the front row of the grid for IMSA cars.

Therefore, NPTI's fastest car qualified by Derek Daly could only start from the third slot, despite recording a time one full second quicker than the pole-sitting Porsche. There was never any intention to run this particular car – effectively a spare – for longer than an hour or so in the race, unless problems hit the other two cars.

Arie Luyendyk, starting in the 'spare car,' actually took the lead on lap thirteen. But it was just for the show, as after Luyendyk's twenty-five lap stint the team restricted this entry to the duty of scrubbing tires for the other two cars. It subsequently dropped its pace and was to complete only forty-seven laps before being withdrawn.

The 'serious' Nissans worked themselves up to the head of the field after a couple of hours' running, with Derek

Daly and Steve Millen at the wheel. They managed to hold on for a while, but then settled into a pattern of trading the position of race leader with the only TWR Jaguar in the race.

All three pace-setters ran into trouble during the night, allowing a Porsche to lead. The lead kept changing hands as the leading runners' fortunes see-sawed. As the sun was rising, Nissan lost one car, when a CV joint broke, causing internal damage to the transaxle and breaking the engine mounts. The other car had still been battling for the lead, but was repeatedly delayed with repairs to bodywork that had been damaged. When Daly hit some debris after midnight, he could only struggle home second.

Frank Jelinski, Henri Pescarolo, Hurley Haywood, "John Winter" and Bob Wollek were the winners in a Joest Racing Porsche 962. Bob Earl, Derek Daly, Chip Robinson and Geoff Brabham were eighteen laps behind in the surviving Nissan. For the rest of their IMSA program, NPTI was to use its own NPTI90 models.

The proudest moment of Nissan's Group C involvement was yet to come, however. The 1992 Daytona 24-Hours was the scene of a concerted attack from the Japanese manufacturer. NPTI again qualified three R90Cs with the intention of running only two. These cars were run in the IMSA GTP category and therefore had to be fitted with downsized 3.0-liter engines. NISMO brought their R91CP in Group C trim, and Nova Engineering also had their R89C in its Japanese spec.

The NISMO car was best equipped to go for a top grid slot and Kazuyoshi Hoshino did set third fastest time to occupy the inside of the second row behind an Eagle-Toyota and a TWR Jaguar. Two NPTI cars were qualified fifth and sixth by Geoff Brabham and Chip Robinson with equal times. Mauro Martini took the Nova car to eighth in qualifying, while Derek Daly put the "reserve" NPTI entry in ninth. Eventually, this car replaced Geoff Brabham's, which sprang a fuel leak in race morning warm-up, so NPTI were down to two entries from the start.

Nissan took a convincing grip of the race from the very start, as Masahiro Hasemi seized the lead at the end of the first lap. Despite its longer pitstops the Japanese crewed NISMO car then stretched its advantage.

Geoff Brabham climbed to second, but his brother Gary brought the other NPTI car's run to an end in the early evening. Exiting the pits on fresh, unscrubbed tires, he slid into the end of the guardrail and wrote off the chassis. The same thing had happened to youngest brother David only minutes earlier at the wheel of a TWR Jaguar, but he managed to continue!

The leading NISMO car was delayed after some seven hours running, when fine sand blocked its radiators. It took some time to discover the cause of overheating, but after the sand had been removed the car ran faultlessly.

The remaining NPTI car's race came to an end just before midnight. Drivers Geoff Brabham/Chip Robinson/Bob Earl/Arie Luyendyk were out with a seized engine.

There were no troubles for NISMO's R91CP, though. From midnight onwards, it extended its advantage and Masahiro Hasemi/Katsuyoshi Hoshino/Toshio Suzuki took an all-Japanese victory, beating the second placed TWR Jaguar of Davy Jones/Scott Pruett/David Brabham/Scott Goodyear by nine laps. Anders Olofsson had been nominated for the winning car, but did not drive, thereby emphasizing the patriotic aspect of the effort. The tires were the only non-Japanese element of the triumph, the team having swapped their Bridgestones for Goodyears for this race.

Mauro Martini/Volker Weidler/Jeff Krosnoff took the Nova R89C to eighth place after suffering a variety of problems, including losing a wheel and braking trouble, which, unfortunately, persisted despite a forty minute stop to change the master cylinder.

R90C:

R90C-01:

1990:
20/5: Silverstone: Bailey/Acheson, #23; NRF.
16/6-17/6: Le Mans 24 Hours: Hasemi/
　　Hoshino/Suzuki, #23; 5th.
23/9: Montreal: Acheson/Brancatelli; 5th.
7/10: Mexico City: Acheson/Brancatelli; 4th.

R90CK/02: Don Devendorf Entry.

1990:
16/6-17/6: Le Mans 24-Hours: Earl/Roe/Millen,
　　#84; 17th.

1991:
2/2-3/2: Daytona 24-Hours: Earl/Daly/Robinson,
　　#83; 2nd.

R90C/03:

1990:
29/4: Monza: Bailey/Acheson, #23; 7th.
03/6: Spa-Francorchamps: Bailey/Acheson,
　　#23; 3rd.
16/6-17/6: Le Mans 24-Hours: Bailey/Blundell/
　　Brancatelli, #24; DNF. (Engine.)
19/8: Nürburgring: Brancatelli/Acheson, #24;
　　9th.
02/9: Donington: Brancatelli/Acheson, #24; 4th.

1991:
2/2-3/2: Daytona 24-Hours: Luyendyk/Bailey/
　　Daly, #1; (Withdrew.)

R90C/04:

1990:
29/4: Monza: Blundell/Brancatelli, #24; NRF.

The garages at Daytona for the 2002 HSR Finale meeting. In the foreground is R90C-03. Behind it is R90C-07. Both cars were being raced in the GTP Thundersports Series and proving very difficult to beat! [Photo: Author's collection.]

20/5: Silverstone: Blundell/Brancatelli, #24; 10th NC.

03/6: Spa-Francorchamps: Blundell/Brancatelli, #24; 10th.

16/6-17/6: Le Mans 24-Hours: Acheson/Grouillard/Donnelly, #25; DNS. (Diff.). NME.

Pole position with Mark Blundell.

7/10: Mexico City: Bailey/Blundell, #23; 2nd.

R90CK/05: Don Devendorf Entry. NPTI entry.

1990:

16/6-17/6: Le Mans 24-Hours: Brabham/Robinson/Daly, #83; DNF. (Fuel.)

1991:
2/2-3/2: Daytona 24-Hours: Bailey/Millen/ Luyendyk, ##84; DNF.

R90C/06: Now an R91CK

1990:
16/6-17/6: Le Mans 24-Hours: Bailey/Brundle/ Brancatelli, #24; DNF.
22/7: Dijon: Bailey/Blundell, #23; 3rd.
19/8: Nürburgring: Blundell/Bailey/Acheson, #23; 5th.
02/9: Donington: Blundell/Bailey, #23; 6th.
23/9: Montreal: Blundell/Bailey, #23; 2nd.
7/10: Mexico City: Bailey/Blundell; 2nd.

1991: Sold to the Nova team.

Used as Spare FromA car.

1992: Uprated to R91CK spec. FromA sponsored.
19/4: 500Km Suzuka: V. Weidler/M. Martini, #27; 2nd.
04/5: 1000Km Fuji: V. Weidler/M. Martini, #27; 3rd.
26/7: 500 Miles of Fuji: V. Weidler/M. Martini, #27;3rd.
13/9: 500 Miles of Sugo: V. Weidler/M. Martini, #27;6th.
4/10: 1000Km Fuji: V. Weidler/M. Martini, #27; DNF. (Acc.)
1/11: 500Km Mine: M. Martini/H-H. Frentzen, #27; 3rd.

1993: Back to Nissan.
2018: In the Nissan museum in Japan

R90C/07:

1991: FromA sponsored car. Built by Lola, Bought from Nissan.
10/3: 500 km Fuji: A. Nakaya/V. Weidler, #27; 2nd.
05/5: 1000 km Fuji: A. Nakaya/V. Weidler, #27; DNF. (G/box.)
21/7: 500 Miles of Fuji: A. Nakaya/V. Weidler, #27; 6th.
25/8: 1000 km Suzuka: A. Nakaya/V. Weidler, #27; 2nd.
16/9: 500 km Sugo: A. Nakaya/V. Weidler, #27; 2nd.
3/11: 800 km Sugo: A. Nakaya/V. Weidler, #27; 10th.

1992: Uprated to R91CK spec.
31/1-01/2: Daytona 24-Hours: V. Weidler/M. Martini/J. Krosnoff, #27; 8th.

1993: Uprated to R93CK spec.
Suzuka: RU.

1996: Sold to Michael Gue, Essex Racing.
1997: Sold to C. Agg.
2004: 12/6: Le Mans: C. Agg; 1st.

2008: Sold to George Purdie.
Good wood Festival of Speed: A. Purdie.

2010: Sold to Steve Tandy.
2012: Le Mans Legends: S. Tandy; RU.
2016: Sold to present owner.
2018: For sale with Bob Berridge, UK.

NOTE: All R91 and R92 cars were updated R89 and R90Cs.

Nissan R90CK Nismo (WSPC 1990)

Chassis	Monocoque in carbon fiber and Kevlar, designed by Paul Bailey, built by Lola Cars, England. 6 built.
Bodywork	Kevlar and Carbon Fiber.
Engine	Nissan VRH35Z 90 degree V8. Four valves per cylinder. 2 x IHI turbochargers
Bore x Stroke	85 x 77 mm = 3496 cc.
Compression	8.5:1.
Power	800 bhp @ 7600 rpm.
Torque	80 mkg @ 5600 rpm.
Electronic Engine Management	ECCS-R-NDIS.
Gearbox	Hewland VGC with 5 forward, 1 reverse gears.
Weight	920 kg.
Wheelbase	2794 mm.
Length	4800 mm.
Width	1990 mm.
Height	1100 mm.
Tires	Dunlop. 13.5 x 18 inch fronts, 15 x 19 inch rears.
Brakes	AP.
Max. Speed	325 kph plus. (Le Mans.)

Charlie Agg has bought the very last Lola-Nissan made and has been campaigning his R90C very successfully in both HSR events in America and Group C events in Europe. Here is a photo of the car immediately after winning the Sebring 3 Hour race in March, 2001. {Photo: Author's collection.]

NISSAN RACING In Japan

5

Of the four Lola T810s built, two were sold to Electramotive in California for their Nissan GTP program, and two were sold to Nissan in Japan for their Group C Program. Here is one of the Japanese Group C cars at Fuji in July 1985 where, driven by Aguri Suzuki, it retired after qualifying in fifth place. [Photo: Courtesy of Nissan.]

Lightning Speed

The Japanese Sports-Prototype Championship took place from 1982 to 1992 and saw some large grids with many Porsche 956s and 962s, both from abroad and from Japanese teams, racing at mainly Fuji and Suzuka. The principal Japanese manufacturers, Nissan, Toyota and Mazda all entered cars through various teams, Nissan using Hoshino Racing, Person's and the Cabin team and then, from 1988, NISMO itself. Nissan had mixed results, Hoshino doing well for them and, later, the NISMO team dominating in 1992 with uprated R90Cs.

In 1983, Kazuyoshi Hoshino and Akira Hagiwara drove their March-Nissan 83G (chassis – 05) into seventh place at the Fuji 1000 kms.

Hoshino and Hagiwara soldiered on in their March 83G Nissan during 1984, but the Porsche 956s had arrived and, as in Europe, they dominated the Championship. Hoshino/Hagiwara's best result was at Suzuka in August, where they placed twelfth.

In 1985, a Lola T810 run by the Central 20 Racing Team, driven by Haruhito Yanagida and Aguri Suzuki, race number 20, appeared at Fuji for the 500-mile race in July, badged as a Nissan and using the

At the Fuji 500-mile race of 1985, Hasemi and Wada drove this March 85G, fitted with a Nissan V6 engine. Although they qualified seventh, various problems dropped them to thirteenth place in the race. [Photo: Courtesy of Nissan.]

Nissan V6 engine. It retired with gearshift problems.

At Suzuka, for the 1000 km race, it retired again with a gearbox problem. At Fuji, in the 1000 km race, the car finished a creditable eighth.

The March 85Gs that Nissan had ordered did not appear until July, when Masahiro Hasemi and Takeo Wada finished a lowly thirteenth at the 500 Miles of Fuji.

At the next race, the World Championship 1000 km of Suzuka, they finished seventh. By now, Hoshino had his March 85G and, at the 1000 km of Fuji, won outright, partnered by Akiri Hagiwara and Keiji Matsumoto. Hasemi and Wada took fifth place at the same meeting.

Thereafter, Hoshino won again at the 1000 km of Fuji with the same co-drivers and Hasemi was fifth. The Lola T810-Nissan of Yanagida and Suzuki placed eighth.

Porsches ruled in 1986, the Nissan-March 86Gs and Lola T810-Nissan having a hard time. At the 1000 km of Fuji, Masahiro Hasemi and Takeo Wada placed third in their 85G behind a Porsche and a Tom's 85 Toyota, and Matsumoto and Aguri Suzuki took fifth.

Those were the best placings, the Nissans usually languishing down the field at the finish or retiring with a variety of maladies.

The only major race that Nissan entered in 1987, apart from Le Mans, was

Masahiro Hasemi. [Photo: Courtesy of Nissan.]

the Fuji 1000 kms. Takeo Wada put the V6-engined car of the Le Mans Company team on pole position; unfortunately, a blow-out with a tire resulted in a lowly thirteenth place finish.

Of the other two factory-entered 87Gs, one went out after just three laps with another tire blow-out, whilst the other finished in 16th place.

In 1988, Nissan redesigned their V8 engine and the rear bodywork of the March-Nissan 87Gs and extended the wheelbase. These cars were known as the R88Cs. In the Fuji 1000 kms, Hoshino, Kenji Takahashi and Allan Grice finished ninth in one of these cars. Paul Bentley, for March, designed the singleton 88G that was V6-engined and it was sold to the Le Mans Company.

There were two of the March 87Gs (Nissan R88C) and the 88G at Suzuka in

122

A rare shot from above of the Nissan-March 86G of Hoshino and Hagiwara at the Suzuka 500 kilometer race of 1986. [Photo: Courtesy of Nissan.]

the FIA World Sports-Prototype Championship in 1989.

Takeo Wada in the 88G with the V6 engine set the third fastest time in the wet and Hoshino and Suzuki finished fourth behind a Porsche and two Sauber-Mercedes but beat the fastest Jaguar.

The Lola-Nissan R90Cs swept all before them in 1990. At the only two races they lost (to the Toyota 90C-V) they were second, with Hasemi and Anders Olofsson winning the 500 miles of Fuji and the 500 km of Sugo.

Hoshino and Suzuki won the prestigious 1000 km of Suzuka. These were all NISMO entries, although a "privateer" Nissan R90V was run by the Cabin Racing Team.

For its 1991 campaign on the All-Japan Sports-Prototype Championship NISMO used slightly modified versions of

Hoshino and Nakago drove this March 86G in the Fuji 500 miles race of 1986 but, despite having qualified in pole position, they were forced out of the race with engine problems. [Photo: Courtesy of Nissan.]

the R90CP. Now dubbed R91CP, the cars could outwardly only be distinguished by an airbox on the rear deck and big rear-view mirrors sticking out from the right hand side upper corner of the windshield.

At Fuji's opening round of the series, Kazuyoshi Hoshino and Toshio Suzuki won from pole despite trouble with a door, which had to be taped shut. Akihiko Nakaya and Volker Weidler were second in Nova Engineering's ex-NME R90CK, just over 1 second behind. Hideki Okada and Takao Wada in a private R89C were fourth.

The second race, too, was at Fuji, and it culminated in a fierce scrap between Toshio Suzuki and Anders Olofsson in the sister NISMO car. Suzuki took another win with Hoshino, but they beat Olofsson and Masahiro Hasemi by only 2.5 seconds after 1000 kms of racing.

Still at Fuji for round three, Toyota got the better of Nissan, but Hoshino and Suzuki stayed at the top of the points table with second place. Hasemi destroyed his car

Matsumoto and Aguri Suzuki shared this Nissan-March 86G in the Fuji 1000 kilometer race of 1986 and came home a creditable fifth overall. [Photo: Courtesy of Nissan.]

in a crash caused by a puncture. He rolled over Takao Wada's Team Le Mans Nissan, which had already been shunted in the same place for a similar reason.

In the Suzuka 1000 kms the leading Nissan spun off in Suzuki's hands after a suspected suspension failure and the race fell to Toyota. Nakaya and Weidler were

The VRH 30 V6 engine, Electramotive built, in the engine bay of a Nissan-March 87G. Sometimes faster than the later Nissan V8 that was used in the Lola-Nissans R89s and R90Cs, the V6 could produce upwards of 1200 horsepower in qualifying trim. [Photo: Courtesy of Nissan.]

second in Nova's R90CK and Hasemi and Olofsson third.

Sugo was the scene of another Toyota victory after Hoshino and Suzuki were severely delayed by a hub failure. Nakaya and Weidler had been the best Nissan crew in qualifying and took the lead at the start, but pitted with the left-hand door ajar. They still finished second, only seven seconds in arrears. Hasemi and Olofsson were third again.

Back at Fuji, Hoshino and Suzuki led most of the way to win a rain-affected race, which was interrupted by five pace-car periods and stopped early.

The Sugo finale was conquered by a visiting Jaguar XJR-14, run on this occasion by the Japanese Suntec F3000 team. Teo Fabi and David Brabham won from the Toyota of Hitoshi Ogawa and Masanori Sekiya. The latter pair came close to winning the Championship, but Hoshino and Suzuki followed them to the flag in third,

Toshio Suzuki drove this March 87G, fitted with the Nissan VRH30 engine, at the WSPC round at Suzuka in 1989. He qualified seventh and finished in fourth place. [Photo: Courtesy of Nissan.]

In 1989, the World Sportscar Championship race in Japan was held at Suzuka. Anders Olofsson and Masahiro Hasemi shared this modified March 87G to take eleventh place overall. [Photo: Courtesy of Nissan.]

which was enough to give them the Drivers' title and Nissan the Manufacturers' one.

For 1992 the Nissans were further modified from the original Lola concept, although there were hardly any outwardly visible differences to the 1991 models. The most important area of change was in the front suspension.

NISMO carried on in the All-Japan Sports Prototype Championship, as did Nova Engineering with the chassis that Lola had supplied them in the middle of 1991. There was also a new Nissan entry from

The start of the WSPC 300 kilometer race at Suzuka in 1990. [Photo: Courtesy of Nissan.]

Nissan: The GTP & Group C Racecars 1984-1993

Team Take One, who had an ex-NISMO chassis in silver colors, carrying number 61 (like Sauber-Mercedes throughout 1989) and modified in the rear along the lines of a 1989 Sauber-Merc! Thomas Danielsson and Hideki Okada were the new team's drivers.

Toyota's effort had been directed in the way of their atmospheric SWC contender, so NISMO had it a bit easier in the Championship, which had its entry depleted just like any other sportscar series in 1992.

Driven by, amongst others, Volker Weidler and Harald Grohs in Japanese Sportscar races, the "FromA" sponsored Lola-Nissan R90CP was very successful. [Photo: Courtesy of Daniel Mainzer.]

NISMO had had a fantastic start to their season, winning the Daytona 24 Hours. Back home, they won a tactical wet-dry series opener at Suzuka. Masahiro Hasemi was now joined by Jeff Krosnoff in the winning car. Hoshino shunted on the first lap and lost 18 laps in the aftermath. A very competitive second was the Nova car of Volker Weidler and Mauro Martini, which had actually led during the wet early phase.

Fuji next hosted a 1000 km race, where the leading Toyotas succumbed to transmission troubles and left the way clear for a Nissan clean sweep. Kazuyoshi Hoshino and Toshio Suzuki won, Danielsson and Okada took second in their "Silver Arrow", Weidler and Martini were third and Hasemi collected fourth with Krosnoff and third driver Masahiko Kageyama after losing several laps with an early visit to a gravel trap.

Fuji was also the scene for round three, and Hoshino and Suzuki won again, using their fuel allowance better than the chasing Toyota of Pierre-Henri Raphanel and Masahiro Sekiya. Weidler and Martini were third, having led early on.

At Sugo, Hoshino and Suzuki simply drove off from the opposition to win by a lap. The other Nissans all had problems, but Hasemi was fourth with Kageyama, as Jeff Krosnoff had injured his leg.

It was back to Fuji next, where Toyota's TS010 atmo SWC challenger beat off the regulars in the hands of Geoff Lees and Jan Lammers. Hoshino and Suzuki were best of the turbos, however, and their second place took the Championship titles out of the reach of their rivals. Lees and Lammers won again at the Mine finale. Kazuyoshi Hoshino was partnered by Takao Wada on this occasion. They took second as the best turbo entry, which gave the Drivers' title to the evergreen Hoshino. Heinz-Harald Frentzen was Mauro Martini's new partner after Volker Weidler's health problems, and the Nova pair capped their season with third place.

1993: The Japanese sports-prototype series collapsed after 1992, but there was a solitary swansong performance for two private Group C Nissans in 1993. Suzuka held its traditional 1000 kms event as an invitation race for a mixed bunch of cars. The only Group C entries were the Nova Engineering R90CK for Mauro Martini and Heinz-Harald Frentzen and a NISMO R91CP for Toshio Suzuki and Takao Wada.

Mauro Martini took pole and the Nova car led for most of the race, but trouble securing its redesigned doors caused extra pitstops and handed the win to Suzuki and Wada. The Nova car was not threatened for second place.

March Group C cars supplied to Nissan

83G/05:
Japan. Nissan LZ20B 2.1 turbo engine.
Kazuyoshi Hoshino.

1983: As Nissan 83G Silvia.
24/7: Fuji 1000 km: Kazuyoshi/Hoshino/ Hagiwara, #23; DNF.
24/8: Suzuka 1000 km: Kazuyoshi/Hoshino/ Hagiwara, #23; DNF.
2/10: Fuji 1000 km: Kazuyoshi/Hoshino/ Hagiwara, #23; 7th.

1984:
01/4: Suzuka 500 km: Kazuyoshi/Hoshino/ Hagiwara, #23; 13th.
03/6: Fuji 500 km: Kazuyoshi/Hoshino/ Hagiwara, #23; DNF. (Fuel.)
29/7: Fuji 1000 km: Kazuyoshi/Hoshino/ Hagiwara, #23; DNF. (Battery.)
30/8: Suzuka 1000 km: Kazuyoshi/Hoshino/ Hagiwara, #23; 12th.
30/9: Fuji 1000 km: Kazuyoshi/Hoshino/ Hagiwara, #23; DNF.
25/11: Fuji 500 Miles: Kazuyoshi/Hoshino/ Hagiwara, #23; DNF. (Diff.)

1985:
07/4: 500 km Suzuka: Hoshino/Hagiwara, #28; 2nd.
05/5: Fuji 1000 km: Kazuyoshi/Hoshino/ Hagiwara, #28; DNF. (Gearshift.)

85G/08: Nissan. VG30. V-6

1985: Run by Hoshino Motorsport.
28/7: Fuji 500 Miles: Hoshino/Hagiura/ Matsumoto, #28; DNF. (Driveshaft.)
25/8: 1000 km Suzuka: Hoshino/Hagiwara, #28; DNF. (Engine.)
6/10: Fuji 1000 km: Hoshino/Hagiura/ Matsumoto, #28; 1st.
24/11: Fuji 500 Miles: Hoshino/Hagiura/ Matsumoto, #28; DNF. (Accident.)

1986:
31/05-01/06: Le Mans 24-Hours: Weaver/ Hasemi/Wada, #32; 16th.

85G/09: Nissan. V-6.

1985: Run by Hasemi Motorsport.
28/7: 500 Miles Fuji: Hasemi/Wada, #11; 13th.
25/8: 1000 km Suzuka: Hasemi/Wada, #11; 7th.
6/10: Fuji 1000 km: Hasemi/Wada; 5th.
24/11: 500 kms Fuji; Hasemi/Wada, #11; DNF. (Accident.)

1986:
06/4: 500 km Suzuka: Hasemi/Wada, #11; DNF. (Engine.)
04/5: 1000 km Fuji: Hasemi/Wada, #11; 3rd.
20/7: 500 miles of Fuji: Hasemi/Wada, #32; DNF. (Fuel.)

85G/10: Nissan. LZ20B-4 engine.

1986: Central Twenty Team.
5/10: Fuji 1000 km: Yananagida/Nakagawa/ Matsumoto, #24; 22nd.
23/11: 500 km Fuji: Yananagida/Nakagawa, #20; 8th.

Lola Group C cars supplied to Nissan

HU-810/03: Le Mans Company (Japan).

1985: Central 20 Team.
28/7: Fuji 500 Miles: Yanagida/Suzuki; DNF. (Shift linkage.)
25/8: 1000 km Suzuka: Yanagida/Suzuki, #20; DNF. (Trans.)
6/10: 1000 km Fuji: Yanagida/Suzuki, #20; 8th.

1986:
06/4: 500 km Suzuka: Yanagida/Nakagawa, #20; DNF.
04/5: 1000 km Fuji: Yanagida/Nakagawa, #20; 6th.
20/7: 500 Miles of Fuji: Yanagida/Nakagawa, #20; DNF.
24/8: 1000 km Suzuka: Yanagida/Nakagawa, #20; DNF. (Diff.)

HU-810/04: Le Mans Company (Japan).
Central 20 Team.
Used as spares for 810/03.

March Group C cars supplied to Nissan

86G/05: R86V Nissan V-6 turbo. Le Mans Company.

New Honeycomb aluminum tub with magnesium bulkheads.

1986: Hoshino Racing Team.
06/4: 500 km Suzuka: Hoshino/Hagiwara, #28; DNS. (Fire.)
03/5: 1000 km Fuji: Hoshino/Takahashi, #23; 8th.
31/5-1/6: Le Mans 24 Hours: Hoshino/Suzuki/Moroni, #23; DNF. (Gearbox.)

86G/06: R86V Nissan V-6 turbo. Sold to Le Mans Company. (Later Nismo.)

1987:
5/10: Mount Fuji 1000 km: Hasemi/Wada, #32; 11th.

86G/07: R86V Nissan V-6 turbo. Sold to Le Mans Company. (Later Nismo.)

1986:
23/9: Mount Fuji 1000 km: DNF. (Driveshaft.)

86G/08: R86V Nissan V-6 turbo. Sold to Le Mans Company. (Later Nismo.)

1986: Person's Racing Team.
04/5: Mount Fuji 1000 km: Matsumoto/Suzuki, #8; 5th.
20/7: 500 Miles of Fuji: Matsumoto/Suzuki, #8; 12th.
24/8: 1000 km Suzuka: Matsumoto/Suzuki, #8; 15th.
5/10: 1000 km Fuji: Matsumoto/Suzuki, #8; DNF. (Engine.)
23/11: 500 km Fuji: Matsumoto/Suzuki, #8; DNF. (Brakes.)

1987: Sold to Le Mans Company. Person's Racing Team.
12/4: 500 Miles of Suzuka: Wada/Olofsson, #8; DNF. (Driveshaft.)
03/5: 1000 km Fuji: Wada/Olofsson, #28; DNF. (Susp.)
13/6-14/6: Le Mans 24-Hours: Olofsson/Ferte/Gonin, #29; DNF.

- 19/7: 500 Miles of Fuji: Wada/Olofsson, #28; DNF. (Accident.)
- 23/8: 1000 km Suzuka: Wada/Olofsson, #28; 21st.
- 27/9: Fuji 1000 km: Wada/Olofsson, #28; 13th.
- 29/11: 500K k Fuji: Wada/Olofsson, #28; 4th.

1988: Italya Racing Team. (Team Le Mans.)
- 11/6-12/6: Le Mans 24-Hours: T. Suzuki/M. Trolle/D. Ongais, #85: DNF. (Engine.)
- 9/10: 1000 km Fuji: Wada/Olofsson, #86; DNF. (Overheating.)

87G/01: NISMO. Nissan V8. Turbo. Group C.

1987: R87E. Hoshino Racing Team.
- 13/6-14/6: Le Mans 24-Hours: Hoshino/Takahashi/Matsumoto, #23; DNF.
- 19/7: 500 Miles of Fuji: Hoshino/Takahashi, #23; DNF. (Accident.)
- 23/8: 1000 km Suzuka: Hoshino/Takahashi, #23; 6th.
- 27/9: Fuji 1000 km: Hoshino/Takahashi/D. Scott, #23; 16th.
- 5/10: Mount Fuji 1000 km: Hoshino/Suzuki, #23; 10th. (86S.)
- 29/11: 500 km Fuji: Hoshino/Takahashi, #23; DNF. (Engine.)

Updated to: 88G/01:
Two built for the Le Mans Company by March. VG 30 V6 Turbo.

1988:
- 11/6-12/6: Le Mans 24-Hours: Olofsson/Leoni/Morimoto, #86; DNF. (Engine.)
- 9/10: 1000 km Fuji: Wada/Olofsson, #86; DNF. (Overheating.)

1989: Cabin Racing Team.
- 12/3: 500 km Fuji: Wada/Morimoto, #85; DNF. (Tire.)
- 09/4: Suzuka: Wada/Morimoto, ##85; 21st.
- 30/4: 1000 km Fuji: Wada/Morimoto, #85; 7th.
- 10/6-11/6: Le Mans 24-Hours: Wada/Morimoto/Olofsson, #32; DNF. (Engine.)
- 23/7: 500 Miles of Fuji: Wada/Morimoto, #85; DNF. (Accident.)
- 3/12: 1000 km Suzuka: Wada/Morimoto, #85; 4th.

87G/02: NISMO Nissan V-8. Turbo VRH30. Group C.

1987: R87E
- 13-14/6: Le Mans 24-Hours: Hasemi/Suzuka/Wada, #32; DNF.
- 03/5: Fuji 1000 km: Hasemi/Suzuki, #32; DNF. (Engine.)
- 19/7: 500 Miles of Fuji: Hasemi/Suzuki, #32; DNF.
- 23/8: 1000 km Suzuka: Hasemi/Suzuki, #32; 22nd.
- 27/9: 1000 km Fuji: Hasemi/Suzuki, #32; DNS. (Driveshaft.)

1988: "R88C" VRH30 engine. 3916 cc V6 Turbo.
- 03/3: 500 km Fuji: Hasemi/Suzuki, #32; DNF. (Elect.)
- 10/4: 500 km Suzuka: Hasemi/Suzuki, #32; 9th.
- 01/5: 1000 km Fuji: Hasemi/Suzuki, #32; 8th.
- 11/6-12/6: Le Mans 24-Hours: Grice/Percy/Wilds, #32; 14th.
- 24/7: 500 Miles of Fuji: Hasemi/Suzuki, #32; 3rd.

28/8: 1000 km Suzuka: Hasemi/Suzuki, #32; 3rd.
9/10: Fuji 1000 km: Hasemi/Suzuki, #32; 12th.

87G/03:
Updated to R88C/03. NISMO.
Le Mans Company. VG30 V-6 Turbo. VRH-30.

1988: VRH30 engine. "R88S" 3916 cc V6 Turbo.
03/3: 500 km Fuji: Hoshino/Takahashi, #23; DNF. (Elect.)
10/4: 500 km Suzuka: Hoshino/Takahashi, #23; 6th.
01/5: 1000 km Fuji: Hoshino/Takahashi, #23; 7th.
11/6-12/6: Le Mans 24-Hours: Hoshino/Wada/ Suzuki, #23; DNF.
24/7: 500 Miles of Fuji: Hoshino/Takahashi, #23; 5th.
28/8: 1000 km Suzuka: Hoshino/Takahashi, #23; DNF. (Gearbox.)
9/10: Fuji 1000 km: Hoshino/Takahashi/Grice, #14; 9th.
Suzuka 1000 km: Takahashi/Scott; 6th.

87G/08:
NISMO Nissan V-8. Turbo VRH30. Group C.

1987:
11/6-12/6: Le Mans 24-Hours: Wada/Marimoto/ Olofsson, #32; DNF?

1988: 3916 cc V6 Turbo. Person's Racing Team.
03/3: 500 km Fuji: Olofsson/Wada, #85; DNF. (Susp.)
12/3: 500 km Fuji: Wada/Morimoto, #85; DNF. (Tire.)
10/4: 500 km Suzuka: Olofsson/Wada, #85; DNF. (Gearbox.)
30/4: 1000 km Fuji: Wada/Marimoto, #85; 7th.
01/5: 1000 km Fuji: Wada/Olofsson, #85; 9th.
11-12/6: Le Mans 24-Hours: Suzuki/ Trolle/ Ongais, # 85; DNF.
11-12/6: Le Mans 24-Hours: Olofsson/Leoni/ Morimoto, #86; DNF. (Engine?)
24/7: 500 Miles of Fuji: Wada/Olofsson, #85; 8th.
28/8: 1000 km Suzuka: Wada/Olofsson, #85; DNF. (Accident.)
9/10: Fuji 1000 km: Suzuki/Morimoto,#85; DNF. (Engine.)

1989: Courage Nissan R 88V.
12-13/6: Le Mans 24-Hours: DNF. (Oil leak.)
23/7: 500 Miles of Fuji: Wada/Marimoto, #85; DNF. (Accident.)
8/10: 1000 km Fuji: Wada/Olofsson, #85; 9th.
3/12: 1000 km Suzuki: Wada/Marimoto, #85; 4th.

R88C/05: (Rebodied from 87G.)

1989:
12/3: 500 km Fuji: Hoshino/Suzuki, #23; DNF. (Engine.)
09/4: Suzuka: Hoshino/Suzuki, #23; 4th.
30/4: 1000 km Fuji: Hoshino/Suzuki, #23; 6th.

R88C/07:

1989:
12/3: 500 km Fuji: Hasemi/Olofsson, #24; 8th.
09/4: Suzuka 480 km: Hasemi/Olofsson; 11th.
9/10: Fuji 1000 km: Suzuki/Morimoto, #85; DNF.

88G/11:

1988:
11/6-12/6: Le Mans 24-Hours: Olofsson/Leoni/Marimoto, #86; DNF.

Nissan R85V Nismo (WEC 1985)

Chassis	Monocoque in aluminum, built by March Engineering, England.
Bodywork	Fiberglass.
Engine	Nissan VG30ET V6, supplied by Electramotive Engineering, USA. Two valves per cylinder. 1 x Garrett turbochargers.
Capacity	2966 cc.
Power	680 bhp @ 7600 rpm.
Torque	70 mkg @ 5600 rpm.
Electronic Engine Management	Don Devendorf designed electronic.
Gearbox	Hewland VG with 5 forward, 1 reverse gear.
Weight	850 kg.
Length	4800 mm.
Width	1990 mm.
Height	1070 mm.
Tires	Dunlop.

Nissan R86V Nismo (WEC 1986)

Chassis	Monocoque in aluminum, built by March Engineering, England. March 86G.
Bodywork	Fiberglass.
Suspension	Wishbone front, rocker-arm rear.
Engine	Nissan VG30ET V6, supplied by Electramotive Engineering, USA. Cast iron block. Two valves per cylinder. 1 x Garrett turbochargers.
Capacity	2960 cc.
Power	700 bhp @ 7600 rpm.
Torque	70 mkg @ 5600 rpm.
Electronic Engine Management	EECP 16/Electramotive.
Gearbox	March with 5 forward, 1 reverse gear.
Weight	850 kg.
Length	4800 mm.
Width	1990 mm.
Height	1070 mm.
Tires	Dunlop.
Max. speed	334.5 kph.

Nissan R87E Nismo (WEC 1987)

Chassis	Monocoque in aluminum honeycomb and carbon fiber, designed by Paul Bentley, built by March Engineering, England.
Bodywork	Fiberglass.
Engine	Nissan VRH35Z 90 degree V8. Four valves per cylinder. 2 x IHI turbochargers
Bore x Stroke	85 x 66 mm = 2996 cc.
Compression	8.5:1.
Power	700 BHP @ 7600 rpm.
Torque	70 mkg @ 5600rpm.
Engine Management	ECCS-R-NDIS.
Gearbox	Hewland VG with 5 forward, 1 reverse gear.
Weight	850 Kg.
Length	4800 mm.
Width	1990 mm.
Height	1070 mm.
Tires	Dunlop.
Max. speed	334.5 kph.

Nissan R88E Nismo (WEC 1988)

Chassis	Monocoque in aluminum honeycomb and carbon fiber, designed by Paul Bentley, built by March Engineering, England.
Bodywork	Fiberglass.
Engine	Nissan VRH35Z 90 degree V8. Four valves per cylinder. 2 x IHI turbochargers.
Bore x Stroke	85 x 66 mm = 2996 cc.
Compression	8.5:1.
Power	700 bhp @ 7600 rpm.
Torque	70 mkg @ 5600 rpm.
Engine Management	ECCS-R-NDIS.
Gearbox	March with 5 forward, 1 reverse gear.
Weight	850 kg.
Length	4800 mm.
Width	1990 mm.
Height	1070 mm.
Tires	Dunlop.
Max. speed	334.5 kph.

Nissan R91CK JSPC 1991

Chassis	Monocoque in carbon fiber and synthetic materials. A development by Nissan of the R90C.
Bodywork	Kevlar and Carbon Fiber.
Engine	Nissan VRH35Z 90 degree V8. Four valves per cylinder. 2 x IHI turbochargers.
Bore x Stroke	85 x 77 mm = 3496 cc.
Compression	8.5:1.
Power	800 bhp @ 7600 rpm.
Torque	80 mkg @ 5600 rpm.
Electronic Engine Management	ECCS-R-NDIS.
Gearbox	Hewland VGC with 5 forward, 1 reverse gear.
Weight	900 kg.
Wheelbase	2794 mm.
Length	4800 mm.
Width	1990 mm.
Height	1100 mm.
Tires	Dunlop.13.5 x 18 inches fronts, 15 x 19 inches rears.
Max. speed	325 kph plus.

Nissan R92CP JSPC 1992

Chassis	Monocoque in carbon fiber and synthetic materials. A development of the R89C.
Bodywork	Kevlar and Carbon Fiber.
Engine	Nissan VRH35Z 90 degree V8. Four valves per cylinder. 2 x IHI turbochargers.
Bore x Stroke	85 x 77 mm = 3496 cc.
Compression	8.5:1.
Power	800 bhp @ 7600 rpm.
Torque	80 mkg @ 5600 rpm.
Electronic Engine Management	ECCS-R-NDIS.
Gearbox	Hewland VGC with 5 forward, 1 reverse gear.
Weight	910 kg.
Wheelbase	2794 mm.
Length	4800 mm.
Width	1990 mm.
Height	1100 mm.
Tires	Dunlop.
Max. Speed	380 kph plus.

APPENDIX

The Electramotive-developed Nissan V6 engine, mounted in 'Elvis' (chassis number 8701). [Photo: Courtesy of Ashley Page.]

To demonstrate the colossal power of the Nissan V6 engine, as used in the GTP ZX cars, here are the tables showing the amount of power and torque developed by one of these engines for installation in chassis number 8701 'Elvis' when sold to Rene Herzog.

Also shown is the specification table for the Nissan GTP ZX 8701.

[Reproduced with the kind permission of Rene Herzog.]

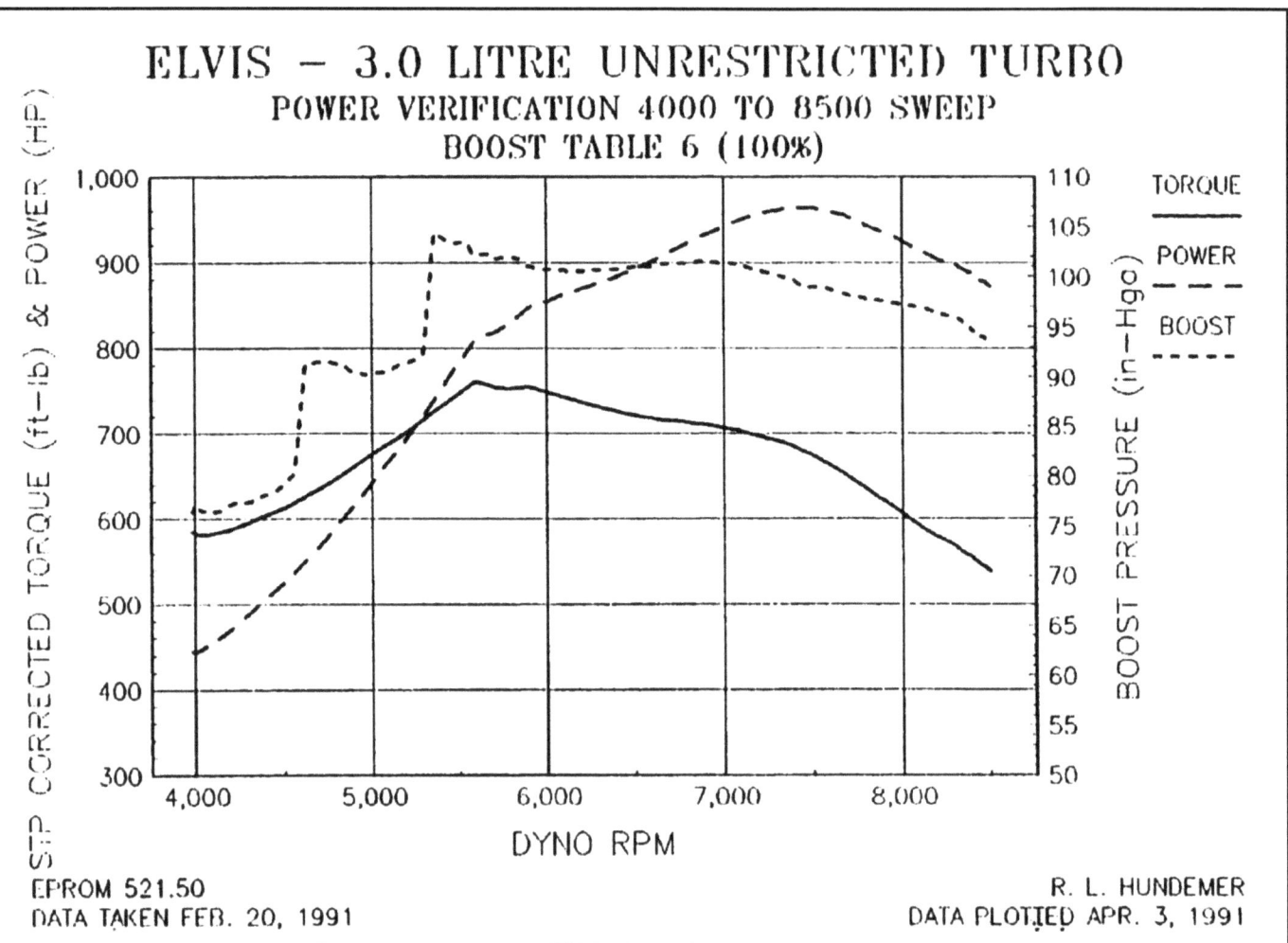

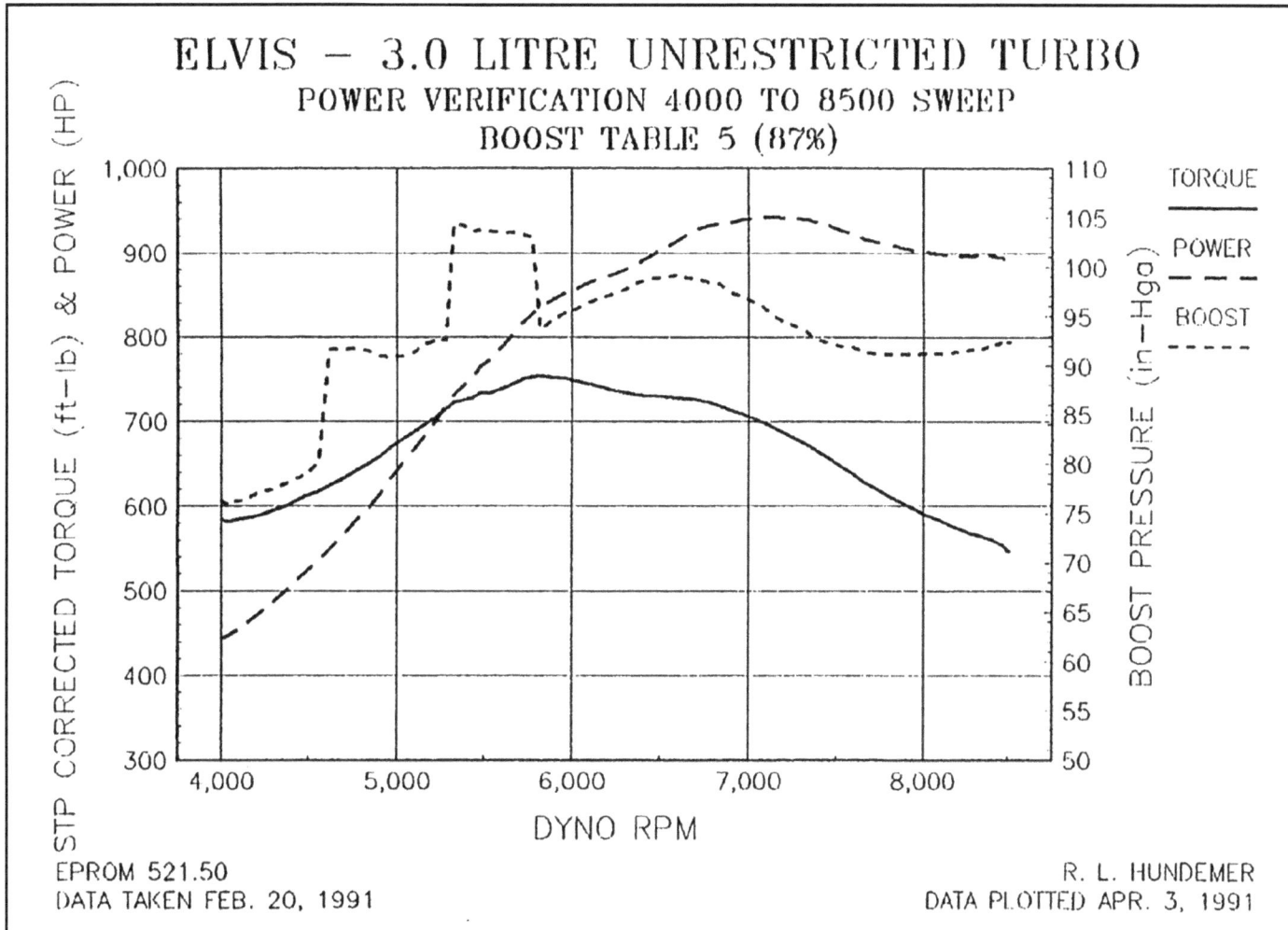

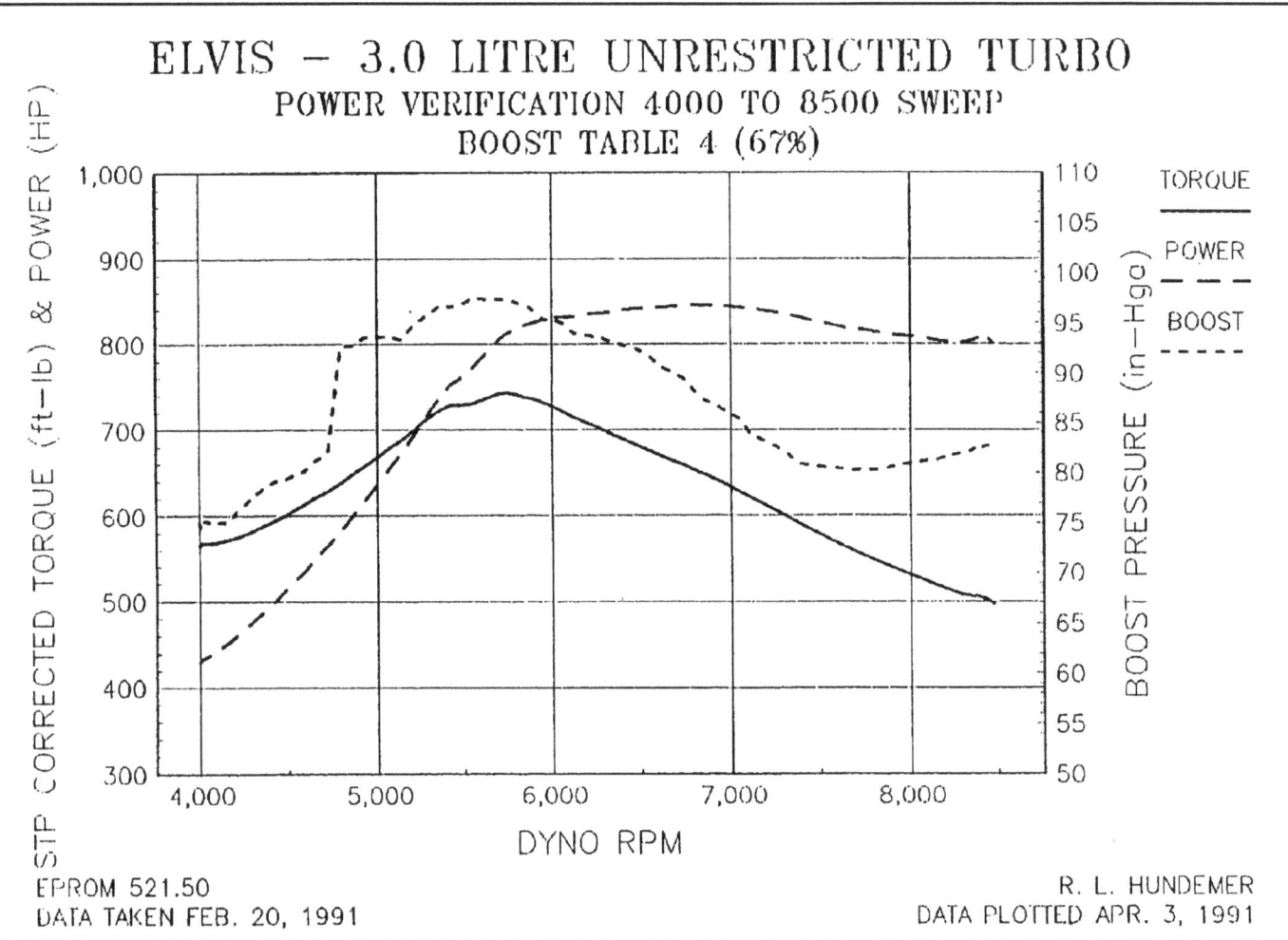

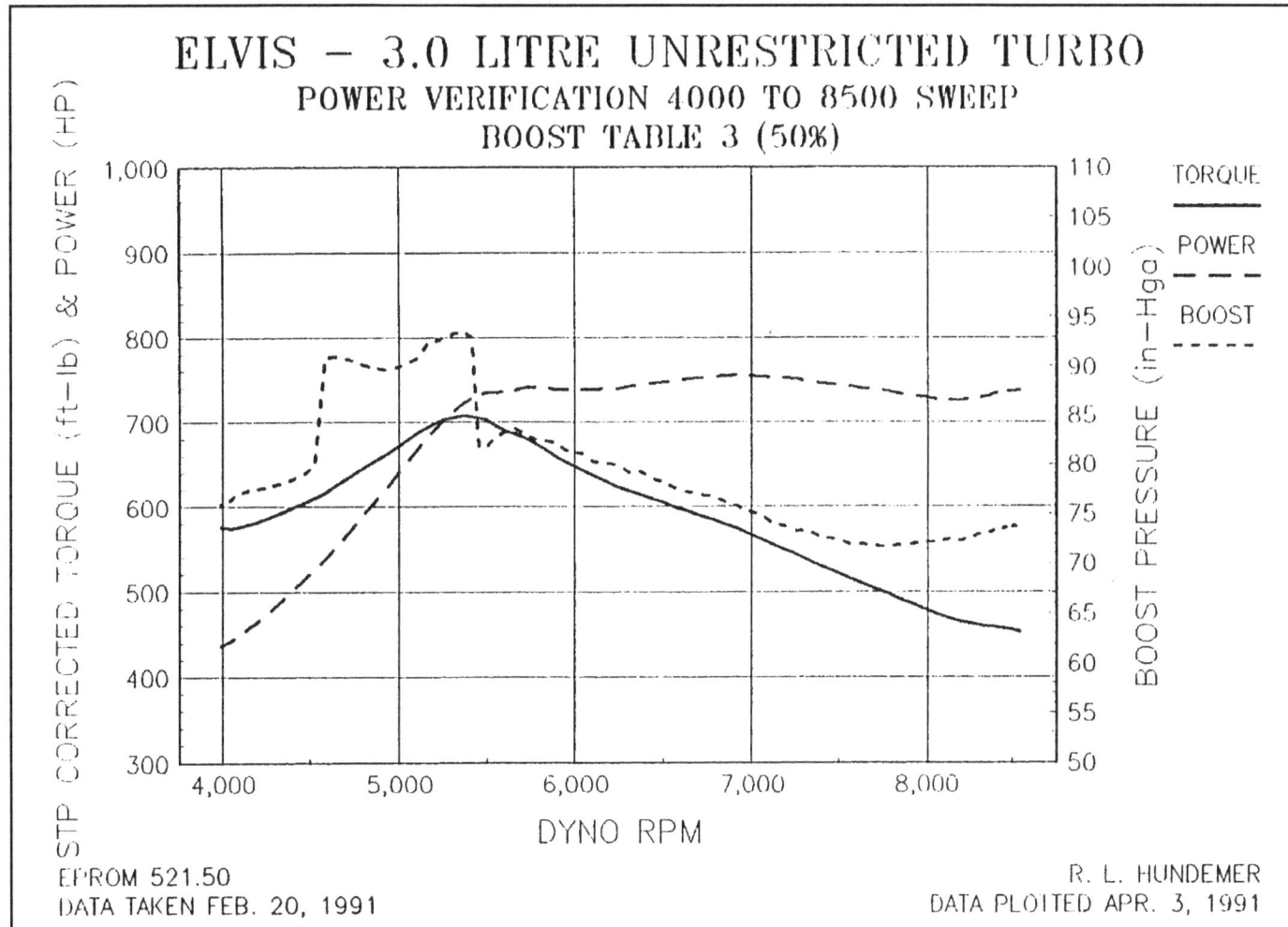

ELECTRAMOTIVE ENGINEERING'S

NISSAN GTP ZX-TURBO SPECIFICATIONS

BODY STYLE	IMSA Grand Touring Prototype, made of carbon fiber and kevlar composite
CHASSIS	aluminum honeycomb monocoque "tub"
SUSPENSION	(front) push-rod suspension with individual A-arms and coil springs. (Rear) suspension also features individual A-arms and coil springs.
ENGINE	Nissan turbocharged V-6, overhead cam, aluminum heads, cast iron stock block prepared by Electramotive, Inc.
FUEL INJECTION	Electramotive Engineering-prepared electronic engine control processor by Don Devendorf
TRANSMISSION	Weismann 5-speed transaxle
HEIGHT	40 inches
WIDTH	79 inches
LENGTH	189 inches
WEIGHT	927 kilograms
WHEELBASE	106.5 inches
FUEL CAPACITY	31.7 gallons
BRAKES	Disc, 4 piston caliper
WHEELS	(Front) 11.5 inches by 16 inches (Rear) 14.5 inches by 16 inches
TIRES	(Front) Bridgestone 23.5 by 11.5 by 16 inches (Rear) Bridgestone 27 by 14 by 16 inches
DRIVERS	Geoff Brabham, Noblesville, Indiana Elliott Forbes-Robinson, Denver, N. C.

# # # #

ALSO BY JOHN STARKEY

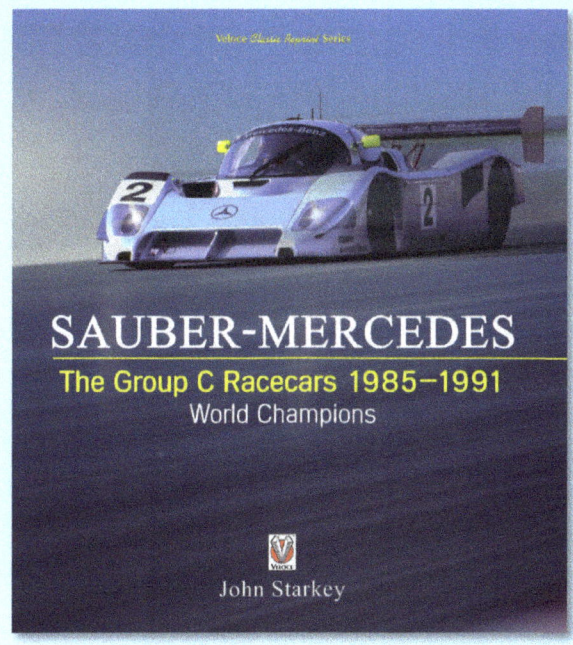

**SAUBER-MERCEDES
The Group C Racecars 1985-1991**

The story of the Sauber-Mercedes racecars that dominated the Group C racing scene during the late 1980s and early 1990s, covering their design and development. This book contains some great colour photos, interviews with many of the best known personalities of the era, and a chassis-by-chassis history of each car.

ISBN: 978-1-787114-93-7
Hardback • 22.8x20.8cm
128 pages • 74 pictures

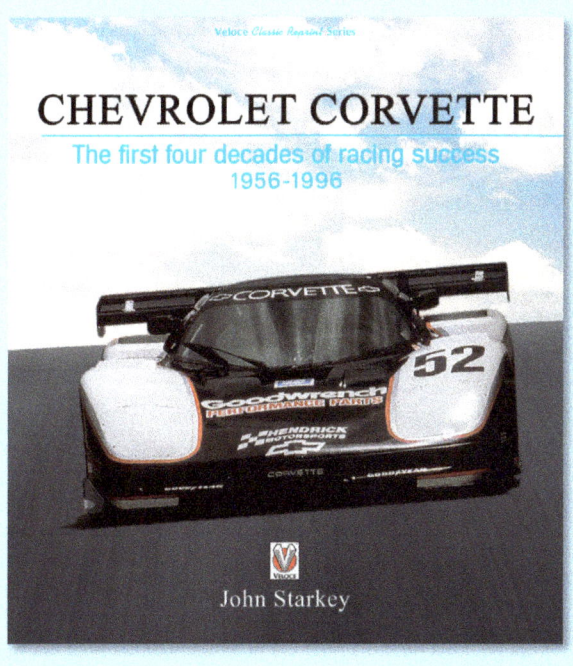

**CHEVROLET CORVETTE
The First Four Decades Of Racing Success
1956-1996**

This book takes a detailed look at the racing Chevrolet Corvette from it's inception, consruction, and it's subsequent updates through the years.

ISBN: 978-1-787114-92-0
Hardback • 22.8x20.8cm
192 pages • 162 pictures

For more information and price details, visit our website at www.veloce.co.uk
email: info@veloce.co.uk • Tel: +44(0)1305 260068

ALSO BY JOHN STARKEY

PORSCHE 930 TO 935
The Turbo Porsches

The complete story of the development of the Porsche 930 turbo, and the racing derivatives of it – the RSR turbo, 934 and 935.

ISBN: 978-1-787112-46-9
Hardback • 23.114x20.828cm • 304 pages • 252 pictures

For more information and price details, visit our website at www.veloce.co.uk

ALSO FROM VELOCE PUBLISHING

LOLA
All The Sports Racing & Single-Seater Racing Cars 1978 to 1997

Back after a long absence! Lola is probably the world's leading manufacturer of racing cars. This book provides the illustrated record of all Lolas built between 1978 and 1997, and tells the story of the Lola company in the same period. A companion volume covers 1957-1977.

ISBN: 978-1-787112-58-2
Paperback • 25x20.7cm • 176 pages

LOLA
The Illustrated History 1957 to 1977

Lola, the British company, is probably the best-known and best-respected builder of racing cars, and has built successful cars for almost every racing formula. This book covers the 63 types of Lola car built between 1957 and 1977, and is written by Lola expert John Starkey, who was curator of the Donington racing car collection.

ISBN: 978-1-787111-04-2
Paperback • 25x20.7cm
192 pages • 176 pictures

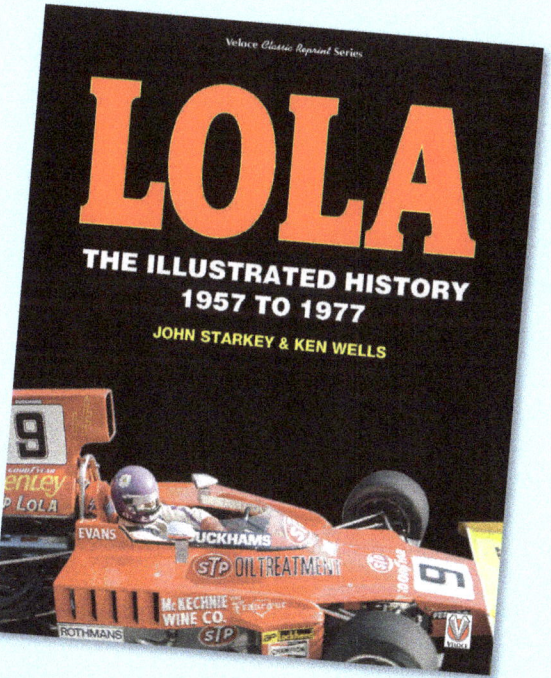

email: info@veloce.co.uk • Tel: +44(0)1305 260068

Also from Veloce Publishing

LE MANS PANORAMIC

The Le Mans 24 Hours is the ultimate endurance race, and a classic feature of the motorsport calendar. This book captures the sheer scale and drama of this legendary race as never before, using specialist panoramic photography to give an unprecedented wide angle view of how the race is entered, watched, won, and lost. It is a timeless tribute to the Le Mans 24 Hours.

ISBN: 978-1-845842-43-7
Hardback • 20x30cm • 224 pages • 118 colour pictures

For more information and price details, visit our website at www.veloce.co.uk
• email: info@veloce.co.uk • Tel: +44(0)1305 260068

www.ingramcontent.com/pod-product-compliance
Lightning Source LLC
Chambersburg PA
CBHW041411300426
44114CB00028B/2979